MEMORIES OF
LEICESTER

TRUE NORTH BOOKS

DEAN CLOUGH

HALIFAX

WEST YORKSHIRE

HX3 5AX

TEL 01422 344344

THE PUBLISHERS WOULD LIKE TO THANK THE
FOLLOWING COMPANIES FOR SUPPORTING THE
PRODUCTION OF THIS BOOK

TS BLOOR LIMITED

DONISTHORPE & COMPANY LIMITED

EQUITY SHOES LIMITED

W FRANK GADSBY LIMITED

GF HAYNES & COMPANY LIMITED

JELSON LIMITED

JS MILLINGTON & SONS LIMITED

NORMAN & UNDERWOOD LIMITED

PAGE & MOY GROUP LIMITED

SAUNDERS OF STAPLEFORD LIMITED

WELLS & ROOT LIMITED

First published in Great Britain by True North Books
Dean Clough
Halifax HX3 5AX
1998

ISBN 1 900 463 08 3

Introduction

Welcome to *Memories of Leicester*, a look back on some of the places, events and people in the town which have shaped the lives of local people over a period of around half a century. The following pages are brought to life by a selection of images from the not-too-distant past, chosen according to their ability to rekindle fond memories of days gone by and show how people used to shop, work and play in the area where they grew up. Modern image reproduction techniques have enabled us to present these pictures in a way rarely seen before, and the lively design and informative text has attempted to set the book apart from some of the other works available.

The Haymarket in the 1950s

The chosen period is one which generally contains events within the memory of a large number of people in Leicester - this is not a book about crinolines or bowler-hats! Neither is *Memories of Leicester* a work of local history in the normal sense of the term. It has far more to do with entertainment than serious study, but we hope you will agree it is none the worse for that. It is hoped that the following pages will prompt readers' own memories of Leicester from days gone by - and we are always delighted to hear from people who can add to the information contained in the captions so that we can enhance future editions of the book.

Many local companies and organisations have allowed us to study their archives and include their history - and fascinating reading it makes too. The present-day guardians of the firms concerned are proud of their products, the achievements of their people and the hard work of their forefathers whose efforts created these long established organisations in the first place. We are pleased to play our part by making it possible for them to share their history with a wider audience.

When we began compiling *Memories of Leicester* several months ago we anticipated that the task would be a pleasurable one, but our expectations were greatly surpassed. There is a growing appetite for all things 'nostalgic' and we are pleased to have played a small part in swelling the number of images and associated information available to the growing number of enthusiasts.

There is much talk in modern times about the regeneration of the local economy, the influx of new industries and the challenge of attracting new enterprise from other regions to Leicester. And quite right too. We could, however, make the mistake of thinking that the changes are all happening *now,* but the reality is that there have always been major developments going on in the city. 'Change' is relentless and the photographs on the pages in the book serve to remind us of some of them.

Memories of Leicester has been a pleasure to compile. We sincerely hope you enjoy reading it.

Happy memories!

TEXT	PEGGY BURNS
COVER DESIGN/PHOTOGRAPH COMPILATION	MARK SMITH
DESIGNERS	MANDY WALKER AND CHRISTINE GALE
BUSINESS DEVELOPMENT EDITOR	STUART GLENHOLMES
COPYWRITER	SARAH PARKS AND MIKE KIRK

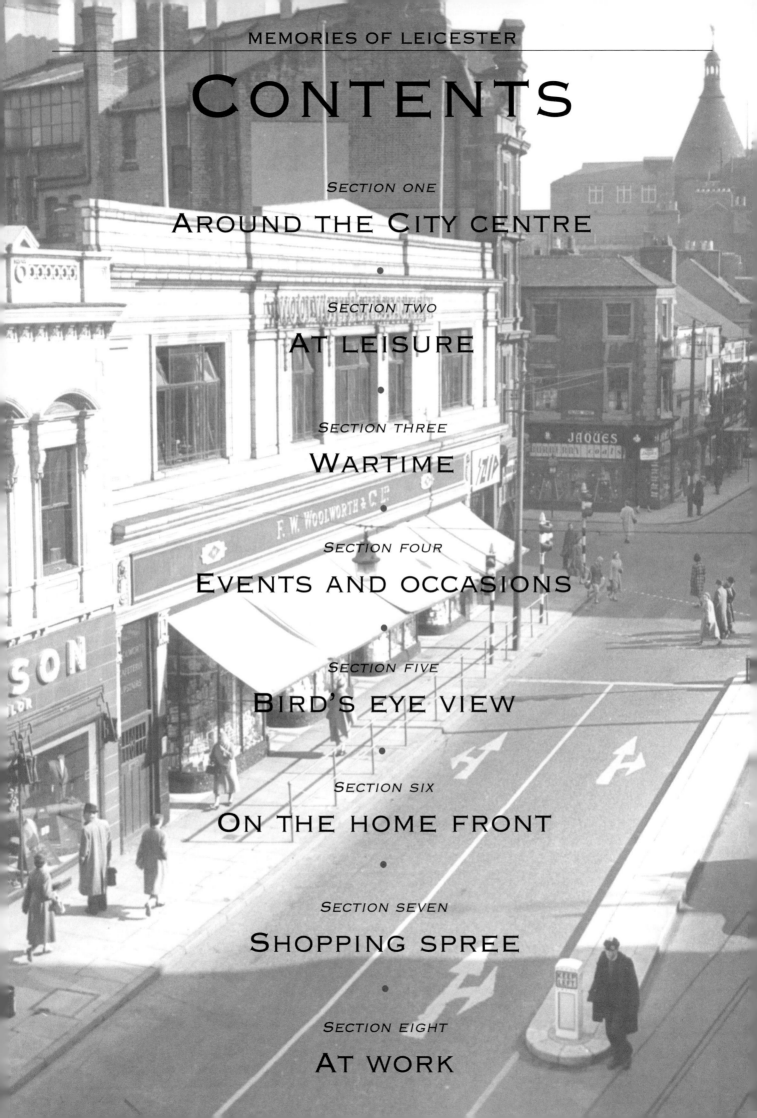

CONTENTS

Around the city centre

Leicestershire Record Office

Pedestrianisation has brought peace to the Haymarket today, but many readers will remember it as it was when this photograph was taken. The area was well known for its shopping, with Lewis's, British Home Stores and Burton's menswear nearby, plus a whole host of smaller shops selling goods of all kinds.

On the left is Cooks World Travel Service that had its origins in Leicester. Today a famous name throughout the world, Thomas Cook, the inventor of the package tour, began his modest travel services in Leicester when he planned local train excursions to Loughborough and Derby.

Other travel companies existed but Cook was the first to offer a comprehensive service; he personally saw to the train hire and the selling of the tickets, and even took an exploratory trip beforehand to check on the cafés and restaurants in the area and the kind of attractions that might interest travellers. He had handbooks printed for each of his passengers that went through the route and listed the landmarks to look out for, and even went along on each trip to make sure things ran smoothly.

Eventually Cook expanded his operations to Ireland, Scotland and further afield.

Leicestershire Record Office

Left: This wonderful pigeon's-eye view of the Haymarket reveals one of Leicester's most best-loved landmarks - the Clock Tower - in all its elegant glory. The mill in the background is the Fielding Johnson Worsted factory in East Bond Street, demolished in the 1970s.

The building of the Clock Tower came about because of a large open space where the Assembly Rooms had once stood in the mid-1800s. This directionless area became notorious because of the number of bad accidents that happened there, and it was realised that a traffic island of some kind was desperately needed. Suggestions included public toilets, a statue or a street lamp, but the proposal the council approved was for a 'bold illuminated clock'. A competition for the design produced 105 entries, and the eventual choice was a design by Joseph Goddard. The foundation stone was laid at a ceremony on 16th March 1886 by photographer John Burton. Only twelve weeks later on 8th June the building was completed, and a dinner was held in the George Hotel to which all the men who had worked on the clock tower were invited. Mr Burton was formally presented with the trowel he had used to lay the stone.

Above: Many readers will remember Lewis's store with fondness; its distinctive tower, seen here in the background, was left standing when the store was demolished. The tower housed one of the city's many air raid warning sirens used during World War II. The buildings to the left behind the Clock Tower disappeared to make way for The Haymarket, Leicester's first shopping precinct. To their right is Burtons tailoring shop, one of four Burtons shops in the immediate vicinity. This branch still survives, though the other three were absorbed by nearby businesses. Richard Shops is next door.

Today the clock tower is so much a part of Leicester that we tend to take it for granted. But its completion in 1868 was a proud day in the life of the town. Not everything ran as smoothly as the proverbial (and appropriate) clockwork, however; building work was already underway when a newspaper rather tardily complained that no time capsule had been placed in the foundations. A bottle with a few suitable enclosures was hurriedly prepared, and together with the topmost stone it was placed on 8th June 1868 by six-year-old George Barfield, the youngest son of the building contractor.

Half a dozen cars and a couple of buses circling the Clock Tower some time in the 1950s would not seem to warrant the high police presence in the area, yet not one but two officers are on point duty at the corner of Gallowtree Gate. High Street goes off to the left and Belgrave Gate to the right.

Traffic did not always flow so smoothly at that junction, however. In the days when it was known as Coal Hill the old Assembly Rooms that stood there were pulled down, creating an empty space that presented a hazard to the horse-drawn traffic of the day, which tended to mill around in a disorderly fashion. After a number of accidents the Clock Tower was built in response to an appeal for some kind of traffic island.

This immediate area was well known for its shops and services, you could be measured for a suit at Burton's menswear, sort out your insurance at the Scottish Legal, call in for quick haircut at Pepperday's Barber's shop on the right, grabbing a packet of cigarettes or a quarter of sweets as you left, then have a quick snack or a leisurely meal at British Home Stores before catching your bus home.

Leicestershire Record Office

Above: 'There is nothing new under the sun' wrote a wise man nearly 3,000 years ago, and his words of wisdom echo around the road works and traffic jams that were as much a feature of our roads forty years ago as they are today. St Mark's church spire presides over this busy scene, recorded in August 1954 when Belgrave Road was being resurfaced. A long tailback of cars, buses and lorries stretches back along the entire length of the road. Nose-to-bumper travel is an aspect of the 1990s that we have had to adapt to, and today even the motorways no longer present the quick getaway they once offered to the commuter.

When the M1 Motorway opened in the mid-1960s it served a valuable purpose in taking the through traffic away from Leicester city centre. It quickly became obvious however that the motorway was causing its own problems - the approach roads were becoming congested with vehicles on their way to and from the motorway. In response, huge areas of the city were swept away to make way for the central ring road, the Underpass and St Nicholas' Circle. An enormous investment was made in the redevelopments - the Underpass, opened in May 1968, cost more than £2 million.

Right: We have no date for this photograph, though the hemlines of the passers-by would suggest some time in the 1950s. Have you noticed that hemlines seem to change with every decade? Wartime fabric shortages led to the knee-length 'new look', while the post-war years and through the 1950s the trend was once more towards the longer calf- length style. 'Flower Power' and the sexual revolution produced the first of the minuscule mini-skirts. Looking southwards along Gallowtree Gate and Granby Street, the elegant tower of the Grand Hotel juts into the skyline in the distance. Granby Street was noted in earlier years for its Temperance Hall, opened in 1853 with Thomas Cook (of travel agency fame) as its sponsor. A keen supporter of the campaign against strong drink, Baptist missionary Thomas Cook first came to Leicester to attend a temperance meeting in the town. The Temperance Hall, used for meetings and public concerts, was very appropriately the first building in the town to receive a supply of pure water from Thornton reservoir. The Natwest Bank on the corner of Belvoir Street also has an interesting history. The Three Crowns Hotel, one of Leicester's old coaching inns, offered good stabling facilities and was a stop-off for stage coaches bound for London.

Still a busy shopping street today, this nostalgic view shows us that Gallowtree Gate was no less so before pedestrianisation; readers may remember buying furniture from Jays or shoes from Hiltons. Readers might just pick out the old four-storey Thomas Cook building further along to the left, where a wonderful frieze above the windows commemorates in charming railway scenes the first half-century of package tours.

Sadly, the flashing lights of the well-loved Bovril advertisement that once decorated the wall of the Scottish Legal Assurance Company has disappeared,

along with the building, whose place was taken by the Alliance & Leicester. Lovers of trivia might like to know that Bovril was first sold as Johnston's Fluid Beef in 1874, and Bovril became the first client of an advertising agency set up by one of Johnston's employees. Within a few years his slogans, not without a touch of humour ('I hear they want more!' says one nervous bull to another), had made Bovril into a household name. The catchphrase 'Bovril prevents that sinking feeling' was designed before World War I but was withheld at the time as a mark of respect for the families of those lost on the 'Titanic'.

Left: This nostalgic view of The Newarke caught on camera in March 1960 gives us a real 'blast from the past'- so much has changed that it is difficult to know where to begin! The traffic sign on the left outside the Newarke Houses Museum directs motorists to turn left to Ashby and Loughborough and right to Uppingham and Welford; this is not of course a through road today. Buses no longer use the road, and the stands on the right where so many commuters waited at the end of a long working day no longer exist. The Barracks of the Royal Leicestershire Regiment beyond were demolished along with the Drill Hall, and the parade ground cleared, and in 1968 the location became the site for the Polytechnic's James Went building, later De Montfort University.

The Magazine Gateway was at one time a thoroughfare, and traffic passed through it until the late 1890s; fortunately the Magazine still stands today, and its only access is via the Newarke subway. Soldiers enlisted for service in the First World War at the Magazine, and souvenirs and battle trophies are on display in what is now the Museum of the Royal Leicestershire Regiment.

Below: The clock in the background reminds travellers that the time is 3.26pm in this nostalgic view of Southgate Street bus station in 1960, and the scene will no doubt stir memories of friends met, journeys made - and buses missed. This bus station is now long gone, of course. Motor buses were first used in Leicester back in 1924, though the last of the city's well-loved trams did not disappear until 1949. Interested readers might like to learn that the Number 76 tram escaped the breaker's yard and was given a new lease of life at Crich Tramways Museum in Derbyshire.

The fascinating old adverts in the background take us back nearly 40 years - and it is interesting to be reminded that Persil was allegedly washing whiter even then. The British public have believed that Guinness was good for them since the drink was first advertised in 1929. Many clever slogans have been produced by the company over the years: 'Tall, Dark and Have Some', 'Seven Million Every Day and Still Going Down' and notably 'I've Never Tried it Because I Don't Like it'. And readers will surely remember 'Guinness is Good for you - Just think what Toucan do'?

Do you remember the 'Hot Potato Man' who always stood in the same position near Swears & Wells on the corner of Silver Street? Those piping hot potatoes were a wonderful comfort to cold fingers on a winter night! Swears & Wells was only one of a number of furriers dotted around Leicester in the days when ladies who wanted to make a fashion statement wore a fur; only in more recent years has the wearing of fur become less acceptable.

Traffic travelling past Lloyds Bank along High Street and into Eastgates was heavy enough when this photograph was taken to warrant a police officer on point duty, though it had a long way to go to catch up to today's frenetic traffic chaos! A Number 27 bus, destination Lime Road, is heading off along Eastgates towards the Clock Tower. This is a picture to stir many memories. Phillips furnishings, and British Home Stores off to the right, are now Laura Ashleys and MacDonalds. Bond Street on the right has been swallowed up by The Shires shopping centre - which in turn has become memorable in its own right, and those who are children today will forty years hence no doubt be asking each other 'Do you remember ...'

FW WOOLWORTH MADE A FORTUNE FROM THE PENNIES SPENT IN HIS POPULAR CHAIN STORES

Gallowtree Gate in 1960 was as popular with shoppers as it is today - only some of the shops are a little different. Going north towards the Clock Tower a large and modern Marks and Spencers store occupies a site on the right hand side of the road, while Boots the Chemist now have the adjoining property. Just off-picture to the right is a popular branch of Woolworths. The first 'Woolies' in Leicester opened as a '3d and 6d Store', with no goods in the shop costing more than sixpence; for the benefit of younger readers sixpence is two and a half new pence! That had to have been a bargain, even in those far off days. F W Woolworth, whose maxim was obviously 'Pile 'em high and sell 'em cheap', made a fortune from the pennies (and dimes) spent in his popular chain stores.

There were a number of shoppers about that day, even on this traffic island, and we can be certain that the small children who make up part of this scene will now be adults with children - and perhaps grandchildren - of their own. How the years fly past!

Leicestershire Record Office

Above: Though most of Gallowtree Gate lies in shade, a low sun highlights the tops of the buildings and dapples part of the roadway and pavement with patterns of light and shade. Though traffic obviously travels in either direction here, we are more used to being able to browse among the shops in traffic-free safety. Pedestrianisation and one-way traffic brought more safety and less chaos to our city streets, though the one-way system was at first rather confusing. The buildings along the left hand side of this photograph that dates from the 1950s are a reminder of the city's much earlier history; they were built on the site of the original eastern wall of the old town of Leicester.

The Bovril advert that flashed its many-coloured message to shoppers in Leicester for a number of years can be seen facing us from behind the Clock Tower. Endorsed by the famous explorer Sir Ernest Shackleton, Bovril gained popularity before World War I, and the company's advertising campaign even ran to flying the Bovril airship up to 1,000 feet above London, where anticipating the war it engaged in mock battles with a biplane.

Leicestershire Record Office

Leicestershire Record Office

to Whiteway's Cyder, who had cornered the prime site. Interestingly, Brown and Polson (of custard fame) were offering free cookery demonstrations at Victoria Hall. Will any reader remember seeing the 'fast and funny revue' being staged twice nightly at the Theatre Royal? Walter Niblo and 'special dances' were featured that week in 'The Laughter Express'. All echoes from the past.

Top: The tall spire of St Mark's church punctuates the far skyline in this view of Belgrave Gate that dates from 1959. The church still stands today, though it no longer functions as a church. Charles Street, which was newly built in the early 1930s, leads off to the right at the roundabout. Declared officially open on 21st June 1932 by the Lord Mayor of London, the generously wide new road ran from Humberstone Gate to Northampton Square. Businesses in the area at the time were John Brookhouse & Co Ltd, leather merchants who had the premises on the left, the Electrical Service Centre and the Midland Dynamo. The area has changed somewhat today of course; in the immediate vicinity off-picture to the right is the Bus station and the Haymarket Theatre, which was opened in 1973, and the Haymarket Centre. The Palace Theatre was at one time Leicester's only professional theatre, and its closure in 1959 left the city without a live playhouse until the Phoenix was established four years later in 1963 as a temporary theatre.

Above: Moving figures smudge the pavement like shades of the long-departed, emphasising the emptiness of a once-bustling thoroughfare where vendors shouted and carts rattled along the cobbles. The exact date of this thought-provoking view of Redcross Street is unknown, but properties were being vacated and numbers six, eight, ten and twelve were already earmarked for demolition. Redcross Street, now part of the rear of the Holiday Inn, has all but disappeared. It once ran from the old bus station in Southgate Street almost to Leicester Castle. Leicester Billposting Co had placed a hotchpotch of choice adverts on the gable end facing us, ranging from a poster calling stridently for disarmament

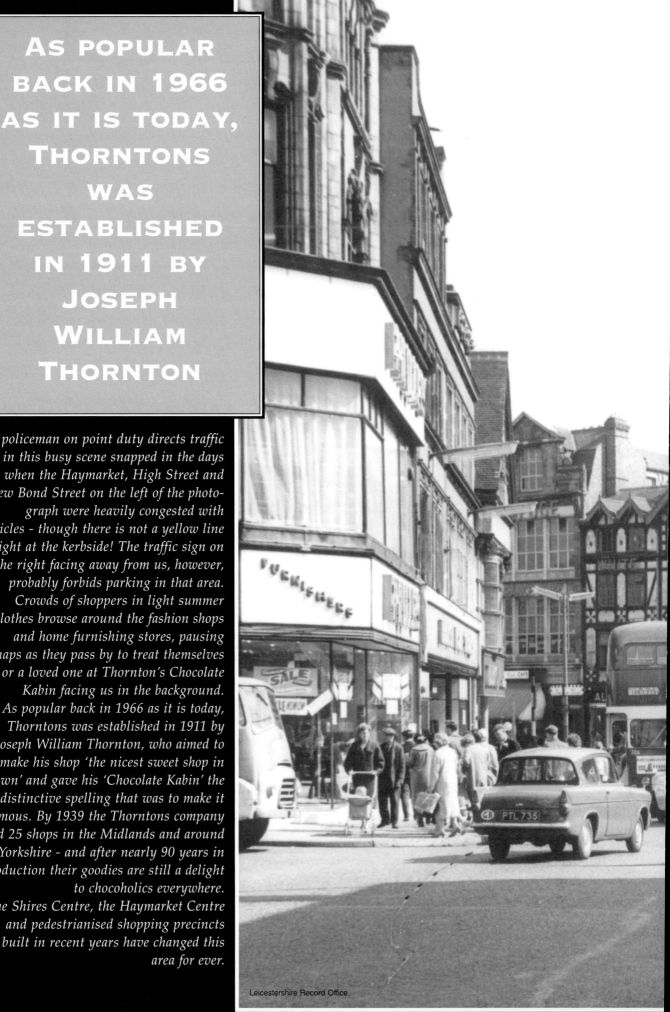

AS POPULAR BACK IN 1966 AS IT IS TODAY, THORNTONS WAS ESTABLISHED IN 1911 BY JOSEPH WILLIAM THORNTON

A policeman on point duty directs traffic in this busy scene snapped in the days when the Haymarket, High Street and New Bond Street on the left of the photograph were heavily congested with vehicles - though there is not a yellow line in sight at the kerbside! The traffic sign on the right facing away from us, however, probably forbids parking in that area. Crowds of shoppers in light summer clothes browse around the fashion shops and home furnishing stores, pausing perhaps as they pass by to treat themselves or a loved one at Thornton's Chocolate Kabin facing us in the background. As popular back in 1966 as it is today, Thorntons was established in 1911 by Joseph William Thornton, who aimed to make his shop 'the nicest sweet shop in town' and gave his 'Chocolate Kabin' the distinctive spelling that was to make it famous. By 1939 the Thorntons company had 25 shops in the Midlands and around Yorkshire - and after nearly 90 years in production their goodies are still a delight to chocoholics everywhere. The Shires Centre, the Haymarket Centre and pedestrianised shopping precincts built in recent years have changed this area for ever.

At leisure

> VANDALISM WAS BY NO MEANS UNHEARD OF IN THE 30S BUT LADS HAD A HEALTHY RESPECT FOR THE LOCAL BOBBIES

This very revealing scene was captured on camera in 1933. The city had recently installed a number of experimental rubber bollards; this one was situated at the junction of Charles Street and Belgrave Gate, and the photograph shows us exactly why the experiment was a failure! Vandalism was by no means unknown in the 1930s, though young children had a healthy respect for the local bobby and teen culture was non-existent. Those early vandals had a long way to go, however, to reach today's level of destruction, where broken glass replaced in a bus shelter might last 24 hours before it is broken again for 'fun'.

The installation of rubber bollards reflected the level of concern about the number of traffic accidents in Leicester. At the time this photograph was taken drivers were not tested on their ability, and a person who had never driven a motor vehicle before could buy a car and drive it away. With far fewer cars on the road, a staggering 120,000 people were killed on British roads between 1920-1940.

The 1934 Road Traffic Act brought in the speed limit of 30mph in built up areas and made driving tests compulsory for new drivers.

Leicestershire Record Office

Left: Cheerful decorations of red, white and blue, coloured bunting and the union flag planted in flowers adorned the city when the coronation was celebrated back in 1953. This photograph shows the Savoy Cinema and indeed the entire length of Belgrave Gate in party mood. Readers will no doubt remember the Palace variety theatre to the left of the photograph, which later became a cinema and was eventually demolished. The Savoy entertained the cinemagoers of Leicester for many years, eventually becoming the ABC. Other uses evolved for the cinema, and at one period God's name was praised from within its walls when it was used by a growing church group who had no building of their own. The ABC's demise was hastened by the growing popularity of television, ironically spurred on by the Queen's coronation as many people bought their first set for the occasion. The pageantry of the event is well remembered by those fortunate enough to have viewed the Westminster Abbey service on TV - it was the first time television cameras had been allowed to film such an important national ceremony, and a sight that few who saw it that day will never forget.

Above: What a brilliant way to get a class of nursery tots across a busy road! This remarkable scene does, of course, raise the question in the minds of those familiar with the unpredictable behaviour of the average three-year-old of how the carers ever got them to keep hold of the rope and each other without physically tying them together. An amazing achievement, and achieved by only two carers to eighteen children which in itself would, of course, be unheard of today, when the ratio is a maximum of five older nursery children to one carer. The law is even stricter with younger babies, where the ratio is three to one. Safety regulations have changed for the better in other directions also, as is demonstrated by the helmet-less motorbike rider approaching the junction. The caterpillar of well-ordered little cuties crossing Sanvey Gate on their way to play on the swings in Abbey Park Recreation Ground was from the Forster Clay's Day Nursery.

This delightful photograph will no doubt make older readers remember and sigh for the days when children of all ages would seem to have been better disciplined than is usually the case today.

Left: Jumping for joy! The pleasure and exhilaration of the moment is captured for ever on camera in this delightful photograph that will surely bring a smile to the face of every reader. The date and place is unknown, though hairstyles and clothing would perhaps suggest the late 1940s or early 1950s. The photograph raises more questions than it answers, however, and curiosity makes us first of all want to know the reason behind the high jinks. Perhaps these girls had represented their school in a tennis tournament and a victory was being celebrated? Or was this exercise simply part of a physical training lesson? We will never know - unless some older reader with children and grandchildren of her own recognises herself and her school friends, and enlightens us! It would be interesting to know what happened to these children; what careers did they follow? What did they do with their lives, and what kind of future did they carve out for themselves?

Bottom left: You can almost feel the suppressed excitement of the crowd in this action-packed photograph, taken in 1945. Greyhound racing was hugely popular with women as well as men, and a vast crowd of eager spectators gathered to watch the racing - and hopefully tuck a few winnings away - that day. A number of soldiers in uniform can be picked out among the crowd, reminding us that the Second World War ended during that same year, with victory being proclaimed in Europe on 8th May and Japan agreeing to unconditional surrender on 14th August. The stadium in Parker Drive was also a venue for speedway racing. Originally termed 'dirt track racing', speedway originated in Australia and quickly established a following in this country. Speedway events proved to be highly popular, and hundreds of fans risked the spitting cinders and crowded into the first few rows to support their favourite riders.

The stadium was demolished during the 1970s, and industrial estates were later developed in the area.

Below: More than one reader who was a child during the 1940s will no doubt remember queuing for the cheap seats outside the Odeon's side entrance on a Friday night. Memories of this cinema also include the wartime notices projected on to the screen to inform the audience that an air raid was in progress outside - and reminding them of the position of the nearest air raid shelter. Few actually left the cinema, however. The Odeon in Rutland Street was still under construction in this nostalgic old 1938 photograph, and when completed the luxurious 'super-cinema' entertained the city's cinema-goers for many years. Television took off in a big way during the 1950s and sadly spelled the end of many of the local cinemas that were dotted around the city. Many fought on valiantly for a few years as bingo clubs or snooker halls. The Odeon came to an unhappy end, as many did across the city when the growing popularity of television badly affected cinema audiences, and the Odeon sadly closed its doors on the last audience and was left to gradually decay. Though the cheerless building still stands derelict and boarded up all is not lost, as more hopeful plans for its future are at present under discussion.

Wartime

Below: War was imminent, and every citizen of Britain, young and old, male and female, was called upon to put his or her back into the war effort. These young boys were not going to be left out; they might be too young to fight but while there were sandbags to be filled and shifted they were going to do their bit to protect the city's buildings. This photograph, taken in 1939, shows young boys working to protect the Central Police Station in Northampton Square - how nice to see the younger generation working along with the police force instead of against them! Wartime often brought out the best in people, and a common spirit of patriotism and the will to win brought communities and individuals together in a new way. Leicester was regarded as a relatively safe place to live during the war; precautions still had to be taken, however, and sandbags were placed around public buildings such as town halls, police stations and schools as a matter of course. It was the industrial towns of the Midlands and the North West that were the prime targets of the enemy, though Leicester did suffer a sustained bombing attack in November 1940.

Right: Thousands of sandbags were used during World War II to protect Leicester's public buildings, and these cheerful local bobbies rolled up their sleeves and got busy. Helped by a group of eager local boys they were on their way to the Central Police Station in Northampton Square with these particular sandbags. Piled up outside doors and windows, sandbags provided excellent cover from bomb blast and prevented windows shattering, and the owners of shops, offices, pubs and on occasions even private houses also resorted to sandbagging their premises. Other people stuck tape in criss-cross patterns across their windows or covered them with net to prevent injury from flying glass should there be an air raid. Leicester was not seen as a prime target for German bombs, and life carried on in the city much as it always had, with cinemas and churches staying open. Even dimmed-down street lighting was allowed in Leicester as the city's position coupled with the usual smoke and fog that hung in the air made it difficult to pinpoint targets from a plane. World War II saw a great pulling-together of the nation. Those who did not go into military service helped in any way they could - and that included Britain's children.

During World War II the citizens of Leicester had grown used to queuing, and queues of one kind or another were an accepted part of life. The war had been over for a number of years, however, when this photograph was taken in the early 1950s, and the men and women in this queue outside A E Piggot & Sons scrap merchants in Red Cross Street were there not to buy but to sell. Their bundles, sacks, carriers and barrows were full of woollen rags which at that time were a valuable source of hard cash.

Even in the 1950s the long looked-for post-war prosperity was still a future dream for the majority of ordinary working class Leicester families. The war in Korea had caused shortages and pushed prices up, and wool had become scarce and expensive. Scrap merchants began to advertise for woollen rags, and were willing to pay good money per pound for them, and in houses around the city cupboards, drawers, attics and cubby-holes were scoured for forgotten old blankets, long-unworn coats, shabby suits, out at elbows jackets and holey cardigans! The rags were later sold on to be processed in Yorkshire.

Left: Blanket-wrapped volunteers were the 'patients' in this Civil Defence demonstration that was staged in Victoria Park at the beginning of the Second World War. In case of enemy attack, it was important for ordinary people to have at least a basic knowledge of first-aid, and this mobile first-aid post provided them with the opportunity to learn what to do if anyone was hurt. How to stop bleeding, treat gas contamination, bandage a limb, treat burns and scalds, dress wounds and treat shock would all have been dealt with.

Before war was declared a little book called 'The Protection of your Home against Air Raids' was sent to every home in Britain to alert the general public to the dangers, informing them of precautions such as preparing a refuge-room and making it gas proof, the importance of blackout curtains, what to do in the event of fire, and most importantly first aid hints. The book's carefully-worded introduction began, 'If this country were ever at war....', though in some quarters there was little doubt that war was inevitable. A list of simple first aid supplies was given, and every home was advised to have lint, cotton wool, bandages and iodine on hand.

Below: Firemen battled to put out fires in Cavendish Road when bombs fell in 1940, causing death and destruction and setting this gas main on fire.

Night after night during 1940 the people of Leicester had listened to the drone of enemy planes passing overhead on their way to drop their deadly load on Sheffield, Manchester, Liverpool and the Midlands. That it was safer to live in Leicester was a recognised fact - ours was a city that received 30,000 evacuees from London, Croydon and Ipswich - more than any other city or town in Britain. Yet Leicester's name was drawn out of the Luftwaffe's hat on 21st August 1940. Air raid sirens failed to sound when this first attack was made on the city by one lone German raider whose target was the gas works in Aylestone Road.

Eight bombs fell, missing the gas works and falling instead in Cavendish Road, where they killed six people and injured many others. When it was all over, the wail of the air raid sirens sounded over the city, giving the citizens of Leicester a tragically belated warning.

Smoke billowing from the Painter's Arms, though appearing to present an emergency, is not a genuine crisis. This large crowd of spectators old and young has gathered to view a demonstration mounted by the local Air Raid Precaution organisation in 1939. Before Britain declared war on Germany on 3rd September 1939 an army of ARP volunteers of both sexes was recruited. At first the ARP personnel were unpaid volunteers but when war broke out in September 1939 they became paid staff.

ARP staff were trained to give help and information to the public, patrol specified areas making sure that

PAINTERS ARMS
FULLY LICENSED

CAR PARK

no chinks of light broke the blackout restrictions, check the safety of local residents, be alert for gas attacks, deal with incendiary bombs, give first aid to the injured, help to rescue victims from their bombed-out properties, clear away rubble, deal with small fires and unexploded bombs and a thousand and one other tasks. The wardens were indispensable, giving their help unstintingly and working alongside the other services to ensure the safety of the public. During the war nearly as many private citizens were killed as troops - and sadly many of them were Britain's gallant ARP wardens.

It was 1939, and war once more loomed on the horizon in Britain. Gas attack was the big fear; Germany had used gas during World War I and they were fully expected to do so again. Well before war was declared millions of gas masks had already been manufactured. People had to be shown how to use them, of course, and the lady on the left of this photograph is receiving some instruction from a good-natured ARP officer. The little girls are obviously not too sure about the new contraptions - children were at first often frightened by the fearsome look of the gas masks, and the very young ones were given blue and red 'Mickey Mouse' masks complete with ears. Babies under two were provided with special gas helmets.

Notices posted everywhere reminded people to carry their masks with them - 'Hitler will send no warning - so always carry your gas mask' emphasised the dangers. At first people carried them wherever they went, but it was not compulsory. Within a few months the fear of gas was receding and gas masks were increasingly being left hanging on a peg behind the front door at home.

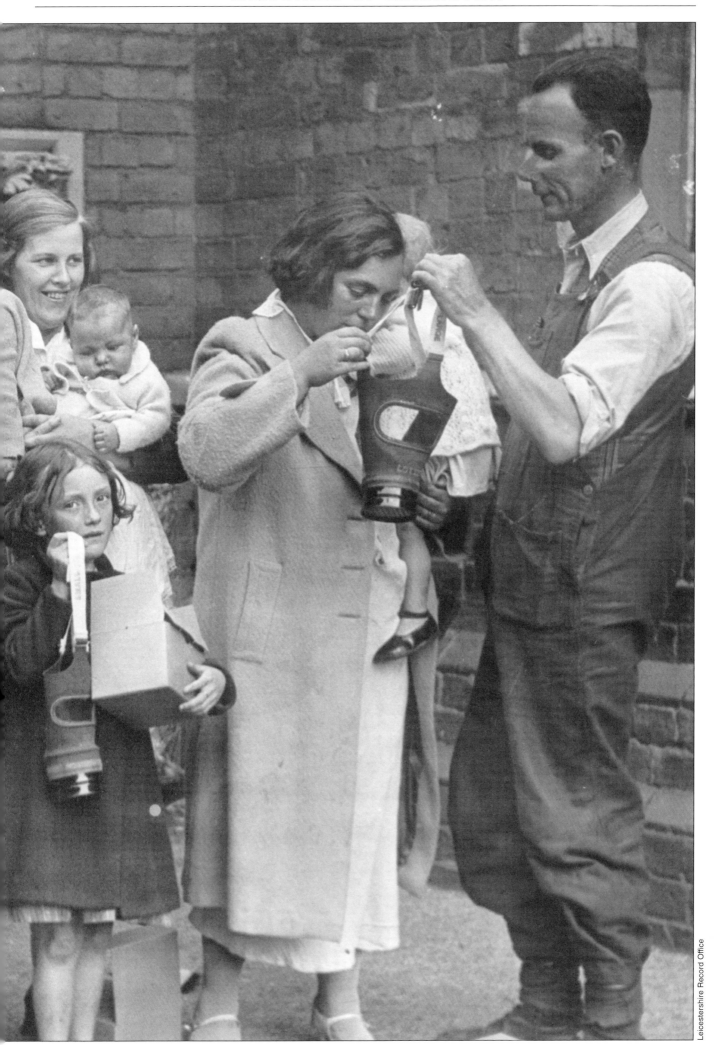

Events & occasions

LEICESTER CITIZENS TURNED OUT IN THEIR THOUSANDS TO CELBRATE CIVIC DAY IN JUNE 1932

Tuesday 21st June 1932 was Civic Day in Leicester - part of Civic Week - and the citizens of the town turned out in their thousands to view the pomp and ceremony when no less a personage than the Lord Mayor of London visited the city. One of his duties in Leicester was to declare the newly-built Charles Street officially open. We know that the original Charles Street, which ran between Humberstone Gate and Northampton Square, was laid out around 1800 as the street appears on a Combe's map published in 1802. The 'new' Charles Street opened by the Lord Mayor was a much wider highway between Humberstone Gate and Belgrave Gate, and was especially designed to take traffic away from the Clock Tower. While he was in the city the Lord Mayor of London also went to see the Leicester Pageant that was being held in Abbey Park that week. The Pageant, which involved hundreds of local people, took spectators through Leicester's long history, daily enacting many of the key events of the last 2,000 years. An announcement on the hoardings in the background advertises the Pageant, though local people must have needed little encouragement to go and view the spectacular event.

Below: World War II was behind them, and hundreds of people crowded into Victoria Park to welcome their Majesties King George and Queen Elizabeth when they paid a visit to Leicester in 1946. The main purpose of the visit was to officially thank the citizens of Leicester for the sterling work they had done for their city and for the country during the war, and particularly to acknowledge their part in providing homes for the 30,000 evacuees who were taken in by local families. The royal couple, seen here with the Mayor and Mayoress of Leicester, had endeared themselves to the people of Britain during the war, when, with their two beautiful daughters Princesses Elizabeth and Margaret, they had lived and suffered along with the rest of the country. The King and Queen showed great courage by staying on in London when they had the opportunity to be evacuated to safety. They insisted that they be treated like everyone else, even to wartime rationing, and the King was almost relieved when Buckingham Palace was bombed - he felt that he could now identify with his people and look them in the face!

Right : Bunting is strung from house to house across the street and patriotic flags snap gaily in the breeze as these children from Muriel Road gather to celebrate the Queen's coronation in 1953 with a street party. Perhaps a few of these children would have been lucky enough to watch the crowning of the Queen in Westminster Abbey on television; it was the first time the coronation of a British monarch had ever been filmed. Television sets were expensive, however, and though Britain had a television service as early as 1936, few people could afford to buy them - and the range of programmes was very limited anyway. By the 1950s sets were beginning to get cheaper, and the Queen's Coronation presented many families with the ideal reason to buy or rent a TV set. Those who did not simply crowded into the parlours of more fortunate neighbours to watch the event! These children who enjoyed the sandwiches, cake, jelly and games on that day so long ago will now be adults with families of their own. What happened to them, one wonders, and what kind of lives did they carve out for themselves?

Bottom: The bowler hats worn by the company managers and civil engineers supervising the reconstruction work were the hardest hats on site when Narborough Road and railway bridge were widened in 1928. 'No hat, no boots, no job' is the slogan that reflects today's emphasis on workers' safety, but 70 years ago employees undertook many dangerous jobs every day without gauntlets, safety glasses, hard hats or protective clothing of any kind, and reflected very little on the risk factor. In fact, in some occupations it was regarded as being somewhat less than macho to wear protective clothing. This road and bridge widening scheme was part of the corporation's programme to create employment in the city. The 1920s were years of national depression and long-lasting unemployment; at the time this photograph was taken 7,500 men were out of work in Leicester. A national Unemployment Fund was created in 1928 - the 'dole' of a pitiful sum that was barely enough to keep alive on, yet infuriating to the well-to-do who saw it as encouraging laziness. Unemployment benefits were cut by ten percent in 1931 and the hated 'Means Test' introduced to examine the personal circumstances of those applying for aid.

Right: Though few events were staged locally to celebrate the Festival of Britain in 1951, the commemorative flower bed being admired by these three young girls was laid out in Abbey Park. Were the girls lucky enough to have been taken by their parents to see the South Bank Exhibition in London? A mere six years after the end of the second world war, the Festival of Britain kicked off the new decade, infusing the country with a spirit of new hope and faith in the future, and the Festival's symbol, designed by Abram Games and picked out here in flowers, was seen in shop windows and around city centres and public places across the country. In London, the cigar-like Skylon, a breathtaking 300-foot high structure, was built as part of the Exhibition; illuminated at night, the Skylon was visible for miles around. The Dome of Discovery nearby was a visible sign of national achievement. The original Festival, staged in 1851 in the purpose-built Crystal Palace, was the brainchild of Prince Albert, Queen Victoria's consort. The 1851 Festival, which promoted British achievements, helped to make the Prince, who was at first regarded with suspicion, accepted and respected by the British.

Leicestershire Record Office

Leicestershire Record Office

Below: A good time was obviously had by all at this fancy dress party held in the Foresters Hall in Rosebery Avenue. Was there a winner? And if so, which of these ingenious costumes won? The cute Mrs Mop complete with bucket? Or was it the jockey, the soldier, or the cowboy? These and all the other clever costumes were probably produced by the nimble-fingered parents of this group of local children. The occasion was the Queen's coronation in 1953, and Leicester really went to town on the celebrations.

The coronation was an opportunity for Britons everywhere to state their patriotism - and an excuse for a country-wide party. The people of every town and village across Britain decked their windows and doorways with red, white and blue garlands, hung bunting across every street, ran up the Union Jack from every flagpole and planned street parties for all the local kids.

The young and pretty new queen was a child herself when she began her training for the throne. She was only 14 years old when she broadcast messages of encouragement to the children of war-torn Britain; she grew up during the war years, gradually taking on more and more public duties.

BENZ'S FIRST ENGINE USED GAS POWER WHICH, ALTHOUGH IT DID WORK, WAS VERY SLOW

There was a lot going on in Leicester in 1953, and the streamers, bunting and patriotic flags outside the railway station and along London Road got a real airing that year. First and foremost, of course, it was Coronation Year. The more local festivities, however, celebrated Leicester Jubilee and the reopening of the Newarke Houses Museum. This procession of wonderful old veteran cars lent an air of genteel sophistication to the carnival atmosphere, their drivers and passengers good-naturedly dressing the part in Sherlock Holmes headgear and 'Genevieve' hats, and no doubt feeling very thankful that the weather stayed fine for the parade. Veteran and vintage vehicles of all kinds were obviously welcome, as further along the line a horse-drawn carriage represented the kind of vehicle that was commonplace before Karl Benz decided to build a carriage that needed neither horses nor steam to make it go.

Benz's first engine used gas power which, though it worked, was very slow. His experiments with a petrol engine succeeded and he produced his first petrol driven motor tricycle in 1885. Horses ran away from the contraption in terror, but that did not stop Benz exhibiting his car at the Munich Exhibition, where it won a gold medal in 1888.

Leicestershire Record Office

Bird's eye view

The busy railway lines and sidings of the LMS Railway Station are the landmarks that immediately draw the eye into this aerial view of the city. The station on London Road was completed in 1892 in response to an increase in traffic at Campbell Street station, where passengers had to walk over railway lines to reach the platform. The problem became more pressing after a fatal accident in 1872. A joint station serving the Great Northern Company's route and the Midland line was discussed but rejected, and eventually the new station on London Road was built. The station offered many modern amenities such as refreshment rooms, a book stall and waiting rooms, which were much appreciated by travellers in those more austere days.

The railway came to Leicester in the 1830s, supervised by the well-known railway engineer Robert Stephenson. His father, the equally famous George Stephenson, drove the first train from West Bridge Station on 17th July 1832. The first passengers, mostly civic dignitaries and company directors, sat on wooden planks placed across the open trucks. The dignity of the occasion was marred, however, when the tall chimney hit a tunnel archway and collapsed, showering the eminent passengers with soot.

Leicestershire Record Office

Left: The landmark that most readers will immediately spot is Leicester Gaol, right in the centre of this aerial photograph that dates from the spring of 1966. The formidable ramparts of HM Prison in Welford Road, complete with turrets, portcullis and arrow slits, have been guarding top security prisoners since it was built in 1828. Less identifiable is the Royal Infirmary in the lower left corner of the picture; over the last thirty years the hospital and the surrounding area has changed almost beyond recognition. A multi-storey car park has replaced the row of houses on the left, and the Infirmary's new Medical Sciences department and other buildings today sprawl out to cover a huge area of land. In the mid-18th Century Dr William Watts promoted the idea of a hospital where patients could be nursed in hygienic conditions, and at a cost of £2,200 the Infirmary opened in 1771 with forty patients and two nurses. The first X-ray machine was installed in 1900. The spire of Holy Trinity church can be picked out on the left, while in the centre near the top of the photograph is Fielding Johnson Hospital, converted from three separate houses. Newarke Museum stands nearby.

Above: Roads spiral off in every direction from Leicester's tall and elegant clock tower, pointing proudly skywards from the centre like the hub of a wheel. To the left of the Clock Tower is the Haymarket and Belgrave Gate, while leading off to the right is Humberstone Gate - here still unpedestrianised. Slightly off-centre to the right we can pick out the white canvas-topped market stalls, with the Corn Exchange nearby. Cank Street to the left of the market led in earlier days to one of the city's most important supplies of fresh water; the Cank well was situated near St Martin's Square. Leading into the picture from the bottom left is Union Street, which together with many of the buildings to its left was swept away to give place to The Shires Shopping Centre.

Many of the buildings on this photograph have gone for ever; a large triangle of old properties between Belgrave Gate and Humberstone Gate was demolished during the 1970s redevelopment scheme. Though the city lost many of its favourite watering holes such as the Stag and Pheasant, the Bell Hotel and the White Hart, it gained the Haymarket Centre and the Haymarket Theatre, opened in 1973.

The 'dog leg' of New Walk and Newarke Street bisect this aerial photograph that dates from 1930, giving us a glimpse back at Leicester as she was. The Midland Railway Station on London Road can be seen in the top left hand corner of the photograph. The Midland line, whose station in Campbell Street originally had only one platform, was the only mainline route through Leicester for 40 years or so. Increasing traffic through Campbell Street called for a new facility and the station in London Road was built and opened in 1892. Welford Road passes HM Prison as it leads off-picture to the right, while below it is Oxford Street and the Royal Infirmary, far more extensive today than back in 1930.

Left of the hospital is the Royal Leicestershire barracks block, drill hall and square, which were later demolished and redeveloped. The nearby Magazine survived the ring road development, and standing in splendid isolation it is today the museum of the Royal Leicestershire Regiment. Originally an ancient footpath, New Walk was laid down in 1785 as a mile-long promenade. Trees and shrubs - supplied by public subscription - were planted along the walk, while gravel for the pathway was provided by the corporation.

This eagle's eye view of the Braunstone estate reveals the amount of space enjoyed by the occupants of these houses - unlike the crowded city dwellers they had space to live, breathe, create a vegetable or flower garden, or pursue a hobby in a shed or outhouse. During the 1930s new houses for sale as well as an increase in the number of council houses available went hand in hand with the city's slum clearance plans. New three-bedroomed homes in Narborough Road were built by the Rossall Building Company, and if you could afford the deposit of £27 and the repayments of 14/8d a week, one of these 'ideal homes' could be yours - and that with no legal charges and no road survey. The full price was £545, and as well as two reception rooms and tiled bathrooms - a real luxury at the time - the tiled kitchenette came fitted with a gas washer.

The power station and gas works can be seen in the background; natural gas reached the city in the 1960s. The same decade also saw the introduction of high rise flats to Leicester when two 24-storey tower blocks were built on Rowlatts Hill Estate.

On the home front

Leicestershire Record Office

Who was this young mother who posed for the camera with her little family in Cumberland Street so long ago? And what prompted the photographer to capture this rather forlorn view on camera? The date of the photograph is unknown, but the cobbled street and the flagged pavement on the right look as though they had at one time been surfaced with tarmac, though badly in need of resurfacing by this time. The boarded-up windows on the left do nothing to enhance what was no doubt, in its heyday, a thriving community - though the rather attractive gas lamp on its bracket in the background is worth a mention.

The photograph was taken from Northgate Street, looking towards Long Lane. The area had a very lively, if somewhat violent, history, when rioting broke out in 1787 in protest against mechanised cotton spinning which of course needed fewer operatives. Master woolcomber Joseph Whetstone, who lived in Northgate Street, escaped the rioters with his life (though without his dignity), by way of a rope from a bedroom window and a borrowed horse.

Leicestershire Record Office

Leicestershire Record Office

prefab bungalows were built in many places; these snug little houses were delivered by lorry and erected quickly on site.

'A house a day' was the target for the New Parks Estate when 162 steel homes were scheduled to be built in 162 days, and to commemorate the tremendous feat, contractors Sir Lindsay Parkinson & Co entertained their workmen on site when the last house was completed.

Left: Construction was barely completed on St Matthew's housing estate when this photograph was taken, but curtains at least one window (plus a television aerial on the roof) tell us that tenants had already started to move in. Built on the site of one of the city's worst slum areas, the new flats and maisonettes offered

Top: It was a red-letter day for this family when they were able to move into their spacious new home in Battersbee Walk on the New Parks housing estate. Each of the new houses had three bedrooms and all modern conveniences including central heating. The lack of sufficient housing had become a real problem in most large towns and cities by the 1920s and 1930s. Many young couples were having to live with in-laws and many districts were overcrowded; though council housing presented a solution for the few lucky families the waiting list was very long. The Second World War, followed by post-war austerity interrupted the city's housing programme, and it was 1955 before slum clearance really got underway. Huge estates were planned at Stocking Farm, Thurnby Lodge, Eyres Monsell, Goodwood and New Parks. Factory-built

modern facilities to the many homeless families. Many have since questioned, however, whether the new council estates, while offering better housing standards, have taken away the neighbourly character of a community. In the early years of this century council housing was a new phenomenon. Two tenement blocks were built near the infirmary in Winifred Street in 1900, and it had been hoped that some of the city's poorest families would be housed there. However, even the comparatively low rents of between three and five shillings a week were beyond their reach. Council houses were a godsend to many - but there were not enough of them, and by the 1950s 13,000 families were on the waiting list. Large estates began to spring up around the city, and in some places prefabs presented a quickly-built solution.

Shopping spree

IN THE 1960S SELF SERVICE SHOPPING WAS JUST TAKING OFF AND SUPERMARKETS WERE SLOWLY BEING INTRODUCED

Takes you back, doesn't it? Many readers will remember the enormous magnet mounted on the corner of Whitcher & Co's store in High Street that was simply known to most as 'The Magnet'. The large branch of the Leicester Co-op just across Union Street was another favoured place with shoppers. Both shops are now long gone, of course, absorbed into the new Shires shopping centre along with Union Street itself, which today forms part of the centre's High Street entrance. This photograph was taken in 1960, when self-service shopping was getting off the ground in Britain and large supermarkets were beginning to establish themselves. Many of the old familiar stores such as Simpkin & James and the Maypole disappeared from the scene, but the Co-op managed to conform to the new direction of shopping, adopting a policy of 'If you can't beat them, join them'. They eventually established hypermarkets in Glenfield and Thurmaston. Carts Lane leads off to the right of the photograph. It is believed that the road could have been given its name in memory of Dr Samuel Carte, who was vicar of St Martins in the early 1700s.

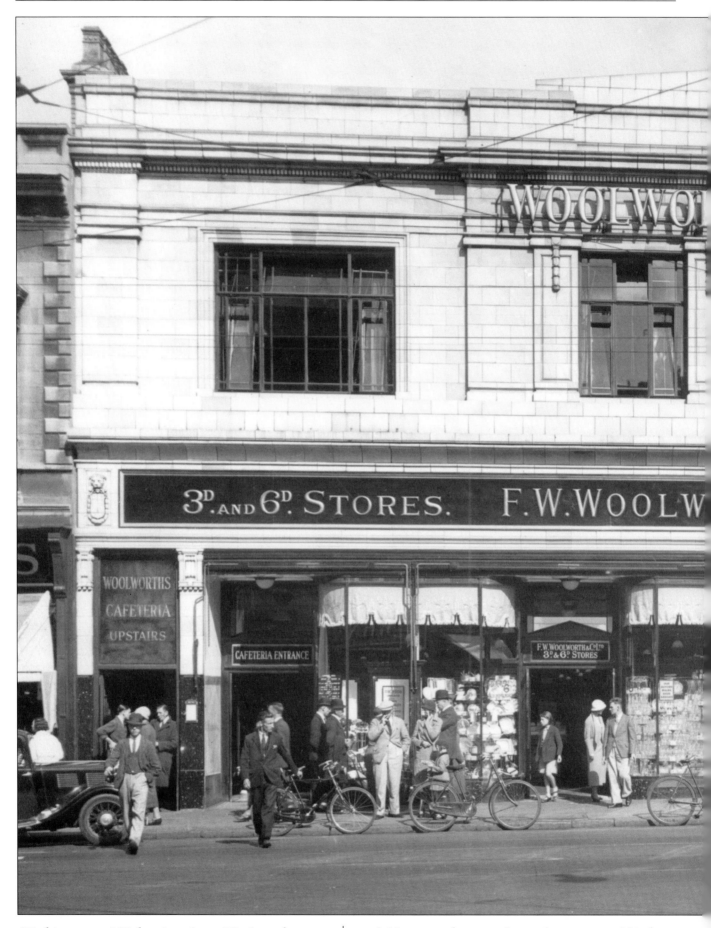

'Nothing over 6d!' the sign above Woolworths proudly proclaims, and the popularity of the store whose prices were pegged can be judged by the number of cycles parked at the kerb.

The multiple windows, so different from the usual layout of today's department stores, are full of useful items such as crockery, glassware and kitchen utensils, and with prices so low the store was invaluable during the dark days of depression and unemployment experienced during the 1920s and 1930s. The Woolworths store in Gallowtree Gate also boasted a large restaurant, and would have been

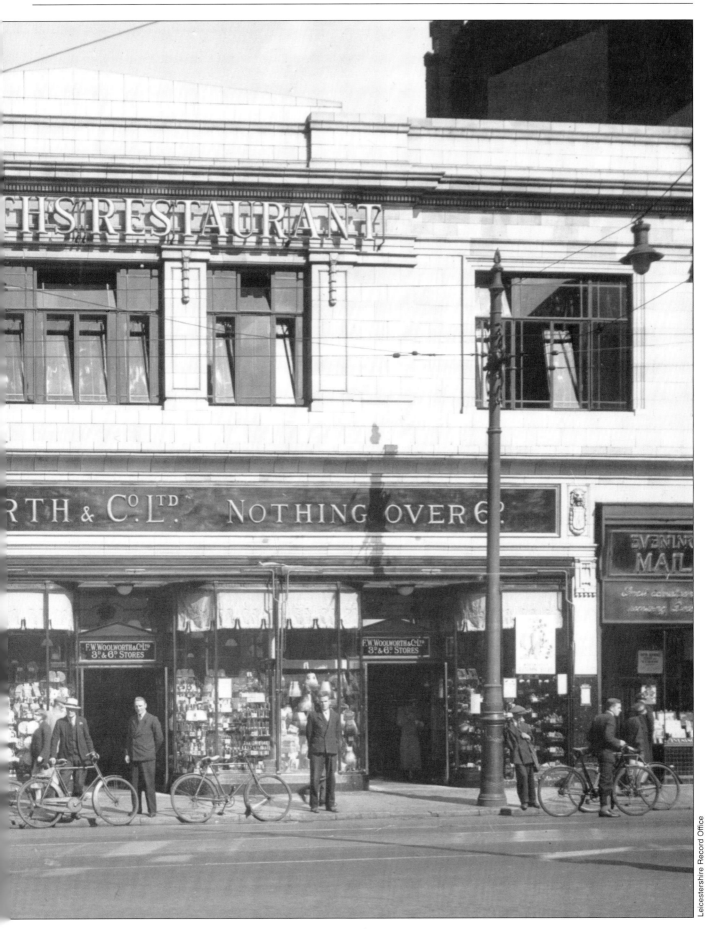

popular with office and shop workers in the city centre. Many thousands of tasty meals must have been enjoyed behind these upper windows, where the food was good and the prices affordable. The Woolworths '3d and 6d Stores' were a direct echo of the original '5 and 10 cent Stores' that spread in a chain across America at the end of the 19th Century. F W Woolworth, who in 1879 opened his first stores selling a wide range of goods at fixed low prices, had a chain of over 1,000 shops in the USA by 1911. With his brother C S Woolworth he later expanded into the UK, Canada and Europe.

Below: The cars in this Wharf Street car park - which no longer functions as such today - would suggest the 1960s, and it was certainly during that decade when supermarket shopping took off in a big way. Many years before that, however, Wharf Street was noted for its excellent shopping facilities; sixty years before late-night shopping caught on across Britain its shops stayed open each Saturday well into the early hours of Sunday mornings. The motorist was well catered for at Tesco's supermarket, with the handy Lee Street multi-storey 'Auto-magic Shopping Park' as well as ground level parking. The petrol pumps between served the motorists' other urgent need. Once known for its crowded slum dwellings, Lee Circle was the site of a number of underground public air raid shelters during the Second World War. Self-service was beginning to catch on by the mid-1950s, and the smaller chain grocers suffered. The trend started slowly, but it was the thin end of the wedge. Gradually many smaller local businesses such as Simpkin & James found they could no longer compete, and one by one they went to the wall.

This branch of Tescos is now used by a sports accessory shop and a ladies and gents fashion store.

Right: Up to 1977 market stalls were allowed in the streets of Leicester, and they were well-patronised by people of all classes of canny local shoppers who realised that the prices charged by street traders were traditionally a few coppers cheaper than the larger shops would demand. Leicester has held a market for more than 1,000 years, though until Elizabethan times market stalls were unheard of, and the market place had no shelter from rain, wind or snow. Traders, farmers' wives, and anyone who had any produce or goods to sell simply went along and laid their wares out on the ground. The vagaries of the British weather caused as many problems back then as the same setup would today, and some time in the 16th Century the corporation shelled out £100 - a large sum of money in those days - to provide market traders with a domed shelter that was supported by eight pillars. Interestingly, the townspeople were forbidden to hang their washing to dry beneath it!

Leicestershire Record Office

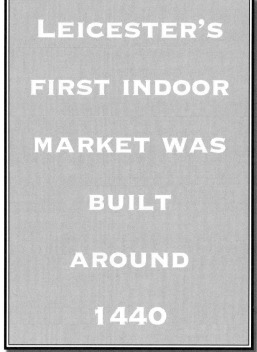

LEICESTER'S FIRST INDOOR MARKET WAS BUILT AROUND 1440

The towers of the Town Hall and of the Corn Exchange preside over this nostalgic market scene, their well-known clocks giving nobody an excuse to forget the time. The greengrocers on the right offers a good selection of fruit, vegetables and salad.

The people of Leicester love a bargain as much as anyone else, and traditionally the open air market (sometimes known as the Saturday Market) was where the bargains were.

When the first indoor market hall was built around 1440 it was ignored by many traders who realised that the best trade was to be had in the open market place. That was where the real life of the town was, with (at varying times) markets for livestock such as cattle, sheep, horses and even pigeons. Entertainment was to be had at the pillory, which was also situated in the market place, and the poor unfortunates sentenced to a few hours' punishment - deserved or not -would suffer the taunts (and possibly the odd bad egg) of those visiting the market. The market place was reconstructed in the early 1970s, and its controversial egg-box style roof has since then provoked a good many love-it or hate-it discussions.

The cry of the rag and bone man will be well remembered by many readers, as they were to be seen around the cobbled streets of our city for a number of years after the end of World War II and even into the 1950s. This delightful scene was captured in 1930, when this rag and bone man was still using a hand cart; by the 1940s the scene had changed somewhat, and most of the merchants had upgraded to the use of a small pony pulling a flat cart. What was the reward given to these small boys for the rags they brought that day? It was probably a free gift rather than a few coppers (hard cash was only given reluctantly!), and the merchant appears to have a selection of gifts ready to give out. The rather tired looking flowers adorning the back of the cart were constructed from feathers and were very likely made by the rag and bone man himself to give as 'freebies' to any small girls bringing their cast-off clothing to his cart. Readers will notice that though their parents are obviously not well off, each of these boys is wearing a stout pair of boots.

At work

Below: Workmen (without hard hats) are here seen hard at work on the construction of St Margaret's Bus Station back in 1939. By the 1960s its facilities were woefully inadequate for the amount of traffic, and it was later demolished. The bus station's second remodelling achieved yet another transformation, and today only those travellers waiting for National Express coaches have to queue outside in the cold. The new bus station offers a range of facilities, and today's commuters can enjoy a quick snack and a cup of coffee, shop for newspapers and sweets, cakes and sandwiches, then join the queue for their local Midland Fox bus, all within the enclosed comfort of this familiar, up-to-date facility. Horse-drawn trams provided Leicester with its earliest form of public transport, though by the early years of the 20th Century rail-laying operations were in progress for the new electric trams. The trams got off to a flying start on 18th May 1904 when the Mayor officially opened the new service and car Number 3, decorated with garlands, left for its very first run to Stoneygate. Motor buses were introduced to the city in 1924, running in conjunction with the tram service until taking over in 1949.

Left: If you couldn't afford the real thing, stockings of artificial silk were a very acceptable alternative - certainly more fashionable than the other option, which was 'lisle', a cheaper cotton yarn stocking that tended to wrinkle badly. Back in the late 1920s, when this busy workshop scene was captured, stocking production - one of Leicester's oldest industries - was in its heyday at A H Broughton & Co. The photograph, though posed, nevertheless shows us how beautifully produced and boxed was the hosiery that left the firm's production line. Low lights over the workbenches help the staff in their work; the young ladies in the background each have an iron to give the garments that professional finish, while the young men perhaps have the job of counting and packing the stockings for distribution. Broughtons had been producing stockings since the firm was established in Bull Head Street, Wigston, in 1911, and they later became part of the Courtaulds Group. Unfortunately the factory had to close down in May 1971 with the loss of 30 jobs - a severe blow to local employees - and production was transferred to Aristoc at Langley Mills in Derbyshire.

Above: Though the identity and exact location of this clothing packaging company has been forgotten, we know that the warehouse was situated in Blackbird Road. All the packers would appear to be women, a sight that by the 1940s had become commonplace. It was during the first world war that women began to take up the kind of jobs they would never have thought of doing at one time. At that time most women stayed at home to raise a family, keep the house clean, and make sure there was a hot meal waiting for her man when he came in from work. Others went 'into service' where they cleaned house for others instead of for themselves. But when Britain's men were called into military service during both world wars, women found themselves performing work that had always been looked on as 'jobs for the men'. Housewives across the country discovered talents and abilities they never knew they had, and developed skills that surprised even themselves. When the war was over many women were reluctant to give up the independence they had found and the fulfilment that had come with going out to work.

Leicestershire Record Office

All kinds of cookery, from baking cakes and bread to learning how to put together a three-course meal, was seen as an essential part of a young woman's education right up until the 1960s. These pupils at the Collegiate School for Girls at North Evington were caught on camera during a housecraft lesson; the large mangle standing against the wall in the background reveals that doing the laundry was another aspect of wifely duties taught at the school. Metalwork and woodwork would have been part of the curriculum of a typical boys' school of the day. It was the bra-burning women's libbers of the 1960s who first

HOW TO PUT TOGETHER A THREE COURSE MEAL WAS AN ESSENTIAL PART OF A YOUNG WOMAN'S EDUCATION RIGHT UP UNTIL THE 1960s

campaigned for equal educational opportunities, equal rights and equal pay, and today's schools offer boys the opportunity to learn to cook and girls the freedom to pursue physics or mechanics.

Mrs Betsey Islip was the Collegiate Girls School's first headmistress. Mrs Islip, a widowed schoolmistress, took over part of a defunct boys' school which after only 30 years in existence had suffered a financial crisis, and founded the new establishment in 1865. The council took over the running of the school in 1922, when it became the Collegiate Girls' Grammar School.

Leicestershire Record Office

Leicestershire Record Office

Above: Well before the beginning of World War II preparations were already being made in towns and cities around Britain for a conflict that everyone hoped would not happen but was nevertheless generally accepted as inevitable. Protection of the people was paramount, and air raid shelters were built around the city centre, at schools and in residential areas - the shelters under construction in this photograph were being built in Imperial Avenue. All over Leicester Anderson shelters were delivered and installed in private gardens, and in public places flower beds and lawns were dug up and air raid shelters built for those who might be caught in the open during a raid. The shelters in Town Hall Square served a dual purpose - the ground around them was turned into allotments where food could be produced.
It was accepted that this war would be different from

previous wars. During the years that followed the Great War of 1914-1918 long range bombers had been developed with the capability of flying long distances carrying a heavy load, which meant that this time there was a real threat from the air. The authorities took the sensible view of preparing for the worst while hoping for the best.

Top: These men harvesting swedes the hard way - one at a time - would no doubt have suffered from backache at the end of this particular day. The wording on the cab door tells us that the location was Beaumont Leys City Farm, though we have no direct information about the farm itself. We do know that the council owned extensive lands at Beaumont Leys on the outskirts of Leicester, prime building land which eventually became the massive housing development that we know today. Beaumont Leys was the site chosen back in 1885 for the largest sewage works development in the country. Prior to 1850 the town had no sewage disposal system at all and was largely dependent on open cesspools that often overflowed and contaminated water supplies and were a breeding ground for a multitude of diseases.
We have no date for this thought-provoking photograph, though it is thought to have been taken some time in the 1940s. The rolling hills of Beaumont Leys (known locally as 'the sandhills') was at one time used as an army training ground. A store of ammunition that had been buried there was discovered many years after the war was over.

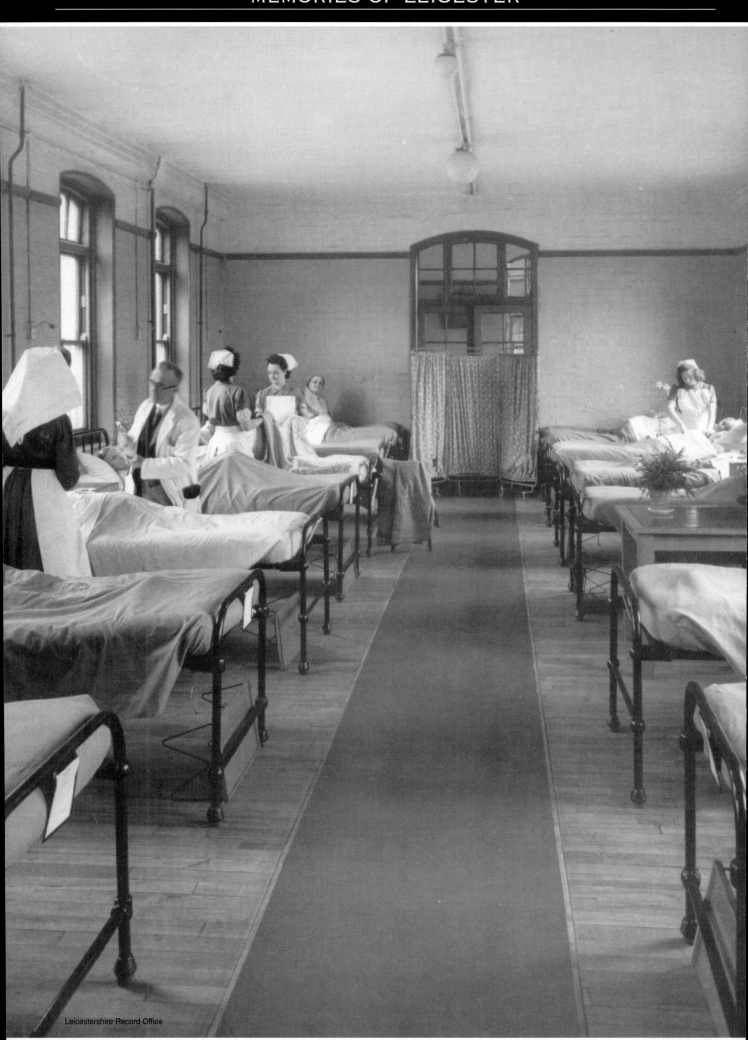

Left: Do you remember the days when a hospital ward was almost as regimented as a military barracks? Matron was the dreaded ogre whose daily rounds created panic among the nurses, who would fly around the ward tidying up, making beds and tucking patients in tightly with a strict warning not to disturb the blankets before Matron's visit. Nurses themselves had to be neat and tidy at all times, and woe betide any nurse whose cap was placed even slightly off-centre! Even the flowers and pot plants in this typical Hillcrest Hospital scene wear an air of clinical formality; which of them would have dared to shed a dead leaf on to the sterile table top? They would, of course, have been removed from the ward at night. Hillcrest was once known locally as 'The Workhouse', where it was said - most unfairly - that once admitted you never came out alive.

The ward sister in her elaborate cap aids the doctor on his rounds on the left of the picture, while further along the ward other nurses are employed in making beds and caring for patients. Hillcrest Hospital was closed in 1977.

Below: This National Fire Service drill was staged, probably in 1939, as a demonstration of the skills of Leicester's wartime services, and it is thought that the group of observers in the background were Aldermen of the city. During the war the National Fire Service took on the control of all civic fire brigades, and women as well as men worked for the NFS. Many women acted as fire watchers; on occasions incendiaries had fallen into unattended office blocks and factories and started fires - a two-hour bombing raid on London just after Christmas in 1940 started a total of 1,500 fires, many of them burning unchecked in city centre properties. After that firewatching became a compulsory duty, and all men between 16 and 60 were called on to organise a fire-watching rota. Later on women between 20 and 45 joined them. The second world war called for volunteers of both sexes to fulfil all kinds of duties, and everyone pulled their weight. The Women's Land Army, the evacuation service and the Women's Voluntary Service sought recruits. Air Raid Precaution wardens were appointed, and men who were outside the age for military service joined the Home Guard.

Leicestershire Record Office

Where did they all go to? Police officers on point duty, that is. There was a time when every major junction in every major town had its traffic 'bobby'; remember those black and white zebra-striped boxes they used to use? The boxes made them highly visible and gave them the elevation and air of authority they needed; the orange-box contraption used by this wartime policeman on duty in Gallowtree Gate is somewhat lacking in that direction. His uniform (note his wartime helmet), which was highly respected at the time, is all this officer needed, however, to set him apart as a figure of authority. Placing police officers on point duty must have demanded a high concentration of manpower, and it was no doubt argued that instead of directing the city's traffic the police force would be better employed in concentrating their efforts on the fight against crime. So a few at a time they departed, leaving the motorist with a legacy of traffic lights to contend with at each junction. Traffic lights, while no doubt keeping the traffic flowing smoothly through our town centres (in theory at least), somehow lack the personal touch provided by the good old British bobby.

Smoothing the road to success

George Frederick Haynes began supplying emery products to the local shoe trade over a century ago in 1897. At this time Britain was the wealthiest nation in the world, despite having a population roughly half what it is today. It was the era before cars were a common sight on our roads, and the year that Aneurin Bevin was born. Bevin would go on to establish the National Health Service some 51 years later.

From the start George Haynes relied upon his sisters, Helena and Kate, to help run the business in the true tradition of small family-run firms. This was the age of the *Suffragettes* and no doubt Helena and Kate would have been interested in the progress being made towards 'votes for women'. It was not until 1918 that women were allowed to vote - and even then this only applied to women over the age of 30!

Initially the business was located in small premises at the rear of Williams Printers in King Street. During the first formative years of the firm the family was also involved in the sale of inking and dyeing machines. Supplying emery products was the major part of the business and initially these were all manufactured by the company. An important milestone was passed in 1907 when George Frederick sailed to America on a Cunard steamship to visit the new Minnesota Mining and

Manufacturing Company. An alliance was formed with the firm (which later went on to become the mighty 3M organisation) enabling George Haynes to become the sole distributor of their emery products to the shoe manufacturers in the United Kingdom. Even now, there is tremendous pride at G.F. Haynes and Company because they have been distributing 3M's products longer than any other company anywhere in the world.

Success and expansion made relocation to larger premises necessary, first to Silvan Avenue and later to Cobden House. Sales benefited greatly during the two World Wars due to demand for military footwear. Close relationships developed with local footwear manufacturers which remain strong today. Over the years the business has developed and expanded into other fields including point of sale and electronics manufacturing, though adhesives, tapes, abrasives and packaging continue to be the core activities of the company.

In the 1950s there were no obvious heirs to the family business and ownership passed to the Bream family headed by Mr Michael Bream. In 1998 a merger with the Walsall company Castle Packaging took place. Designed to strengthen both firms' abilities to serve the technical and practical needs of their customers by pooling resources and learning from decades of experience built up at each company. Links with 3M are as strong as ever and products are continually improved to stay ahead of the competition. George Haynes would be proud to see the progress that has been made.

Above: *The founder, George Frederick Haynes with his wife, children and the nanny.*
Left: *Haynes' trade stand at Granby Halls, Leicester in 1910.*

Family foundation

The story of Jelson Limited, and its rise to prominence as an award-winning house-builder, regarded today as one of the leading employers of the East Midlands, is a tale of family endeavour, self-reliance, a commitment to crafts-manship and, perhaps most of all, to an abiding bond of loyalty between management and workforce. 'Once a Jelson man, always a Jelson man' went the phrase, and even today, when long service with a single employer has become all but a thing of the past, nearly 100 staff can boast over 25 years uninter-rupted experience with the firm. The roots to this remarkable state of affairs go back a long, long way.

In 1889, James Jelley, the 24 year old son of an engineer was living with his wife at 43 Shenton Street, Leicester and decided to set up in business on his own account as a self-employed joiner and shopfitter. Operating from his home, the business soon prospered and by 1897 employed seven staff. Extensive travel was a strong feature of these early days, as James began to generate work - principally in shopfitting - throughout the region. His diligence paid off, and as joinery and shopfitting contracts started to flow in, the business was able to offer a growing range of services. By the early 1900s, James Jelley was also making a name for himself as an undertaker. In the years that followed, Shenton Street was enlarged to cope with increased amounts of activity - stables at the rear of adjoining houses were developed to house a machine shop on the ground floor and a joinery workshop above, while the firm was also able to acquire stores on the other side of

Shenton Street, in addition to a funeral parlour and shop in nearby Charnwood Street.

Above: Herbert Jelley, son of the founder (James Jelley) started working in the family business in 1919.
Below: One of Jelson's developments during the 1940s with its own fleet of machinery and transport.

A more fundamental growth in the company's fortunes accompanied the arrival at the firm of James' son. Herbert Jelley served with the Leicestershire Yeomanry during the First World War, in White Russia for a time, and had also received a grounding as an apprentice with a Leicester firm of builders and joiners. Discharged from the army in 1919, he shortly afterwards began to work with his father and almost immediately showed a keen aptitude for the building business. With his sister, Florence (later Mrs Stubbings), at his side - taking responsibility for office work and sales - Herbert soon had a building operation up and running. Early projects consisted of single houses, or pairs, in the Humberstone area of Leicester - and under Herbert's able stewardship, the new venture was soon flourishing, while his father continued to concentrate his efforts on the joinery, shopfitting and undertaking side of the business. By 1925, J Jelley & Son were already firmly established as a sought-after local builder employing around 40 staff in the joinery shops and on a growing number of building sites.

Herbert lived in Greenland Drive in Leicester and is remembered as a forthright yet fair individual, much respected in the local community. He was apparently a 'stickler for good time-keeping' but inspired unfailing loyalty amongst the workforce by many acts of kindness and a genuine concern for their welfare. Every Friday afternoon, he would visit all the sites with a Gladstone bag and personally hand out wages to each of the men, and when one employee, Walter Wincott, was keen to buy his first company-built house in 1934, Herbert even arranged

to guarantee his mortgage. While the depression hit many firms in the 1930s, J Jelley & Son continued to prosper - through a combination of benevolent management and an unrivalled reputation for dependable, high-quality workmanship.

If Herbert was a model employer, he was also a businessman of considerable acumen and enterprise. By the late-1920s, the local authority was increasingly turning to J Jelley & Son for the construction of Leicester Corporation housing estates; but Herbert was looking ahead and becoming interested in the scope for private housing development. With characteristic foresight, he began a process of land acquisition, seizing opportunities to purchase parcels, a few acres at a time, for future building schemes on the outskirts of Leicester. A ready market for private housing was further enhanced by forging productive links with local building societies, and within a few short years J Jelley's own housing construction became the firm's main activity. Before the outbreak of war in 1939, annual output had risen to 400-500 properties on a number of sites, the largest being at Wyngate Drive/Hinckley Road. The average price at that time for a typical semi-detached house was in the region of £375 - while a weekly wage for an apprentice was around 10/2d (51p) for a 48 hour week.

Above: Florence Stubbings who with her brother helped towards building a successful business.
Left: The original premises at 43 Shenton Street, Leicester.

New home-owners in the mid-1930s were demonstrating a modern appetite for self-reliance and a relish for independence and autonomy in their lives. J Jelley & Son, meanwhile, were beginning to manifest a similar philosophy in their approach to business. As their house-building activities grew, so the joinery division in Shenton Street expanded until it was eventually able to supply all the major timber components used in Jelley houses. Herbert's purchase, in 1932, of the firm's first mechanical excavator also marked the start of a process that would lead eventually to the current modern fleet of internal plant, enabling the company to tackle virtually any on-site task without recourse to subcontractors.

By 1939, the business had set its course for the future. By now, it was predominantly a housebuilder, with other departments given over almost entirely to supporting that role. Although some shopfitting was still undertaken, the funeral parlour had to be disposed of. There was an atmosphere of exciting change and new beginnings - but it was also the end of an era, made all the more poignant by the death in 1938 of James Jelley. He worked assiduously right up to the end, at the heart of an enterprise he had himself founded - very nearly fifty years before. If there was any immediate comfort for his loved ones it was that at least the company itself would survive, under the able command of his son, Herbert.

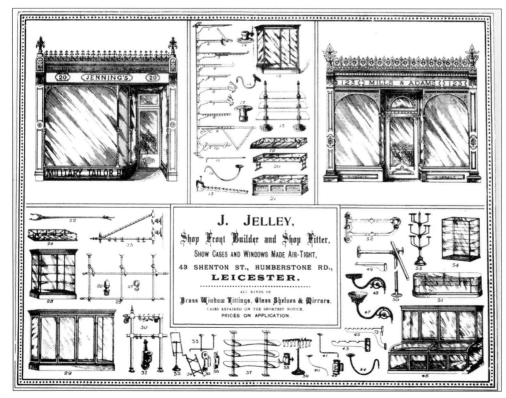

War broke out - and everything changed. Mortgage funds dried up as building societies ceased lending and J Jelley & Son found themselves at work on houses for which there could be no buyers. There was only one solution and that was to let them, as

Above: Some of the employees that were the driving force of the joinery works.
Left: An advertisement of the original range of shopfitting work that the firm made.

they were finished, in order to recoup at least some of the building costs until they could be sold. It's an interesting fact, however, that some of those lettings survive to this day - an odd little feature in the company but a tangible reminder of wartime vicissitudes.

Private housing development ground inevitably to a halt, and many Jelley staff were called up for military service - but it turned out to be a busy few years for the company. Factories in the Midlands were turned over to essential war work and J Jelley & Son were soon actively involved in maintenance and reconstruction tasks on industrial sites throughout the region. Bombing raids wrought devastation in a number of towns, and J Jelley & Son were able to supply gangs of skilled workers throughout the war to assist with rebuilding. At one point, the firm had 80 men travelling by lorry from Leicester to Coventry each day, and 40 to Nuneaton. Unusual jobs during this period included the construction of stands for the visit of King George VI and Queen Elizabeth to inspect the war damage - and the building of the first two British Restaurants in Coventry, where people could enjoy a meal for about one shilling (5p). In Leicester, meanwhile, the firm - using its own agricultural equipment - converted some of its sites at Narborough Road, Wigston and at Scapcroft for crop production!

Business remained brisk, and varied. But there was tragedy too when Herbert's elder son, Leonard - already a member of the firm - was killed in Burma in 1944. It therefore fell to his younger brother, Ronald, to continue the family tradition and he joined the company as an apprentice joiner as the war came to an end. Herbert's immediate objective, at the end of hostilities, was to resume normal business activity as quickly as possible. Florence, still active at her desk, wrote innumerable letters to all former staff who had been on military service with a single request: 'when can you start back?'. And men returned in their droves at the first opportunity, to set about a host of projects which mushroomed as peace returned. Repairing war damage was a vital task in Leicester as in so many other towns after the war, and although the government imposed an embargo on private housing development, there was huge investment targeted on Local Authority housing schemes. J Jelley & Son won several large contracts to build houses both in the city and in the county as a whole. One of the first major jobs was the construction of a hundred houses at Woodhouse Eaves to provide homes for workers - some from Cyprus - who had been recruited to the War Department Signals Depot at Garrats Hay.

By 1947, with a loyal and industrious workforce in place, a turning point was reached for the business when a private limited company was formed to take over the assets of the family firm. This significant step was accompanied by a change of name - and from this time onwards, the business has been known as Jelson Limited. A new era was over the horizon, and the next decade was to see the company making dynamic strides forward under its chairman, Herbert Jelley. Whilst the embargo on private housing construction persisted, the company tendered successfully for other projects, including work on schools, factories and offices. This experience was to provide a useful background to diversification in the

Below: Club Members at the Quarter Century Club dinner in 1988, with the chairman seated in the centre.

modern era, but in the early 1950s - when private housing schemes were again permitted, Jelson fell to the task with renewed enthusiasm. Expansion across the East Midlands saw a growing workforce required on a number of different sites, and the company was swift to purchase buses to move labour to Uppingham - and later to purchase vans based in Uppingham for use in Peterborough and Stamford. At one time, it was said that Jelson had 'more buses than the Corporation!'

It was soon apparent that the Shenton Street premises were inadequate to support the new levels of business activity. In 1957, work began on its present headquarters at 370 Loughborough Road, accommodating on its three acre site a modern office block, a purpose built joinery unit and a depot for a growing fleet of plant and vehicles.

By the 1960s, Jelson Limited had become a building force to be reckoned with. Operating from its Leicester base across some 26 sites spread into Rutland and Lincolnshire, the next 20 years saw the number of completed houses reach 10,000 units in the 1960s and 9,000 in the 1970s. Smaller house and bungalow developments were now only part of the story, as Jelson embarked on a number of architect designed properties in higher price ranges. Commercial and public customers also increased in number with a variety of major building and civil

engineering projects coming Jelson's way. Self-reliance remained a company characteristic - as it does today - and was typified at this time by the supply of sand and gravel from Jelson's own pits - four of which were brought into operation in Leicestershire in the early 1960s. While other builders were slimming down their direct labour forces, Jelson's own saw a period of expansion and the workforce grew to 750.

When Herbert Jellly died, after a period of illness, in 1963, the reins were taken up by his son, Ronald who successfully steered the business to still greater success. The completion of the Leicestershire village of East Goscote was a notable achievement. Conceived as an entire community, and unique in its day, it was based on a 140 acre site, between Queniborough and Rearsby. Formerly the home of a government munitions factory, and subsequently a store, Jelson acquired the land by auction and then set about the elaborate job of demolishing all the old buildings and developing and landscaping the site to provide a full range of village amenities - including a school, shops, pub, village hall and industrial units.

Above: An example of the latest type of architect designed property built by Jelson.
Left: A view of the Jelson Group premises in 1989 at 370 Loughborough Road, Leicester.

In more recent years, innovative projects have embraced the refurbishment and conversion of older properties for the modern lifestyle. A particularly interesting example has been the Parklands development in Sleaford, on the site of an ancient Roman burial ground and mint, which included the refurbishment of an historical manor house - the 'Old Place' - reputedly haunted by the ghost of Lord Hussey who was executed in 1538. Nothing untoward is believed to have occurred in the course of this work! - and the result is a remarkable celebration of our historic past achieved by means of the most modern building techniques.

Jelson Ltd celebrates its own proud traditions too and continues to place the greatest emphasis on the importance of people. The family atmosphere, for which the firm is renowned, remains as inspirational today as it has always been - and great store is still laid by long service. The company's Quarter Century Club, which has as its members both retired and current staff boasting over 25 years employment with the firm, has become a popular forum for reminiscence and renewed friendships and each November a dinner in Leicester sees new members welcomed, each one presented with an inscribed gold watch.

With Ronald's sons, Robert and Graham Jelley, already occupying senior positions in the firm, the future looks assured, and the old motto 'once a Jelson man, always a Jelson man' is as true today as it ever was.

Above: The current chairman of the company, Ronald Jelley, who was presented with a clock in 1989 from Bill Farmer on behalf of the members of the Quarter Century Club to the only one of their number, who's service had not been recognised with an award.
Below: A building site in Matlock with Robert and Graham Jelley discussing business.

Well on track

In May 1997 Wells and Root proudly celebrated seventy five years of successful trading as a family business. Like so many of the best things in life the company came about almost by accident. Ernest Wells, on the advice of his doctor, left his job as a swim-wear designer in the textile industry to work out of doors. He had set up his own wet fish round when he met his future partner Bert Root, a packing case maker. The two decided to combine their talents in the production of packing cases, shook hands on it and went from strength to strength. Such a simple start is not uncommon but those that succeed so well are but a small percentage of those that set out. Ernest's fishmonger's bell is still kept in the company offices!

The new company of two partners and a boy, Ernie Hall, established the business, Wells and Root, in a former stable in Clarendon Park Road. Ernest Wells was the ideas man, Bert Root the craftsman and young Ernie delivered the finished products on a handcart. In the 1920s handcarts and horse drawn vehicles were much more common than motor traffic. In a family company of this nature traditions are as important as standards and the remembrance of Mr Wells, dressed in the ubiquitous bowler hat and carrying a walking stick, travelling to work by public omnibus is treated with respect and affection by a firm which is sure of its place in the world. Managing Directors who work on the shop floor, with their

sleeves rolled up, a pencil behind their ear and glasses tipped forward on the end of their nose, in the style of Bert Root, win the respect of a happier workforce than remote pen pushers can ever achieve.

It was not an easy road to success as the family remember the times following large deliveries of timber when Mrs Wells had to make do without her housekeeping money, which had been used to pay for stock in trade! Young Ernie Hall, one of life's pessimists, remained convinced that his job was insecure until the day he retired after fifty four years with Wells and Root. Their neighbours in Clarendon Park Road were Bentley Engineering a company later to become well known world wide. The first case supplied to them was to export an earth driven clock, later for the

Above: Working outside the factory in 1947 at Devonshire Road.
Left: Wells and Root's, Parker Drive, premises in 1954.

komet sock machines and the larger circular knitting machines, many of which are still working today.

Wells and Root survived the 'Depression' years to move to larger premises in Devonshire Road in the 1930s when they took the step of registering as a Limited Company. The difficult years of World War Two saw Wells and Root continuing their box making as vital 'war material'.

Many companies had to change dramatically from peacetime production to 'war work' but Wells and Root were fortunate in being able to cater for the enormous demand for packing cases of all kinds. Their speciality was the padded boxes required for delicate radar and radio parts.

Following his 'demob' from the RAF, Bernard Jack Peach, a former flight engineer in flying boats who had finished his war as an instructor, joined the company on its reversal to peacetime trading. Although married to Mr Well's daughter, Gwen, he started at the bottom doing manual work on fourteen

hour shifts. Its not all beer and skittles when you work for your in-laws, let alone for yourself! On his own initiative he took his 'demob suit' to work so that he could change in order to see potential customers. Post war expansion saw Wells and Root move in 1954 to larger premises in Parker Drive where they are today, albeit in a much extended

Above: Loading up the lorries inside the factory in 1954. Below: The Belgrave Road station, picturing a consignment for export in 1964 to Korea.

building. Bert Root had already retired when without any warning, let alone celebration to mark the end of an era, Ernest Wells, sixty five in June 1957, simply cleared his desk at Saturday lunch time and left, never to return.

A year later his son Jack joined the firm and worked with his brother in law to expand the firm's operations in the heady days of the fifties and sixties. Together they invested heavily in new equipment, including a five ton overhead crane, to assist the crating of irrigation and generating gear destined for the developing world. In 1963, when Jack Wells became joint MD with Jack Peach, the former became responsible for purchasing and production while the latter took charge of sales and administration. Sadly Jack Wells died in 1969, after barely serving a decade in his father's firm, leaving Jack Peach to carry on.

He was joined by future son-in-law Graham Langley who worked his way up the company ladder, in the same hard working fashion employed by Jack Peach, to become MD in 1983.

The company were well established as shipping agents for sea borne freight when, in the late 1960s, Jack Peach led it into the air cargo field as East Midlands agents for Air Express International of New York and Philadelphia. This new venture involved the conversion of part of the Parker Drive factory to cater for air freight packing. This bold statement

barely hints at the impact such complete diversification to new untried aerial operations had on the development of the company when pioneering such an addition to an established sea-going business. To switch horses from one, which was about to decline from pre-eminence, to another, then considered revolutionary, calls for courage and vision beyond the norm, which Jack Peach had in abundance.

During this exciting period Neville Welsh joined in 1968 as a trainee case maker. He progressed through all the departments gaining knowledge and experience in all aspects of the company and in 1996 he became the first non-member of the family to be appointed director. No doubt others will follow in the firm's tradition of working their way from the shop floor to management positions. The company is doubly strengthened by encouraging a loyal long-service work force and by enjoying the undoubted benefit of their in-house expertise.

Today Wells and Root offer their clients the services of an international freight forwarding company which is unique in providing not only professional in-house packaging but the complete transport and documentation service too, making exporting easier for their valued clients. The customer's property is safely cared for from pick-up from factory to delivery to a

Below: The first container that went through New York Port Authority.

WELLS & ROOT LTD

point anywhere in the world. Staff are so well trained that company drivers are very security conscious, an important factor in a world beset by industrial sabotage, aerial hi-jacking and insecure governments in some of the world's more volatile market areas.

That this world is still as exciting a place as in the days of flying boats and horse drawn delivery vans is proven by some of the transit problems which Wells and Root routinely resolve for their customers. Amongst the unusual consignments have been the transport of canned beer for construction engineers working in the teetotal deserts of Middle East oil fields, and then who would dream of air-freighting milk bottles to test the capabilities of a French bottle washing plant! Even today some items must be packed in containers suitable in size and weight to be forwarded by pack mule, dug-out canoe or even on the heads of native porters. It is not unusual to export English made prayer mats to the faithful in the Indian sub-continent but would you believe that Wells and Root's books record the carriage of sand to Saudi Arabia?

Another traveller's tale is that of hiring a Hercules air freighter which crashed at Calcutta homeward bound from Hong Kong. Unperturbed Wells and Root hired another, then standing in Alaska, to complete the job with no more than forty eight hours delay. A costly way of keeping customers happy and maintaining a hard won reputation. It once took eight weeks to ship goods to Australia and New Zealand and four days by sea to New York, these journeys, immeasurably speedy though they would appear to travellers in the days of sailing ships, have been reduced to one day to the Antipodes and an unbelievable four hours across the wide Atlantic Ocean.

Wells and Root are confident that their progressive company will lead the way into the new millennium. Just imagine the company records will soon be showing the transition from handcart to space ship within the lifetime of two generations. Now there's something for the ambitious lads in the design team to get their teeth into!

Above: The modern premises of Wells & Root with a history of seventy six years of trading.
Left: Large water storage tank starts the first leg of its journey to a third world country.

Putting you in the frame

The term 'picture frame' has generally come to mean the rectangular structure, made of wood, metal, or any synthetic material you care to name, that surrounds a picture or mirror. But this is a pedestrian interpretation of what can be, and is often intended as, an indispensable means of enhancement of both picture and the space in which it hangs. The twin crafts of picture framer and gilder have for centuries contributed to our appreciation of works of art and for the last hundred years have flourished at the heart of the firm W Frank Gadsby Ltd of Leicester.

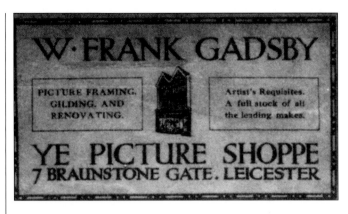

In the 1890s, after serving his apprenticeship at Langdon's in Waterloo Road, young Frank Gadsby was employed as a junior picture framer and gilder at the Advanced Picture Framing works on Narborough Road. As his confidence grew in newly-acquired skills, he proved himself able in the intricacies of preparing wooden moulds, applying ornament, sizing and gilding. In 1900, at the age of 25, he requested a pay rise of sixpence a week. It was refused and with exemplary aplomb - and not a little audacity - he walked out and started his own business in a shed at the bottom of Marquis Street. His only furniture was a bench in one corner and a piano in the other, and his only hope - to prove himself quickly.

Frank's first commission came not a moment too soon, but it was a gargantuan task: to regild Trinity Church in just three days. The young man was not going to be beaten and worked day and night to complete it.

Above: Examples of Gadsby's early advertisements that have contributed to the company's success.
Right: A portrait of Mr W. Frank Gadsby, who founded the company in 1898.

It was an achievement that earned him instant respect, and before long further commissions arrived.

Frank's wife, Susannah Basford, whom he had married in 1898, was soon drawn into the business herself and their six children were all born over the first shop at 7 Braunstone Gate. It survives today as the hub of the Gadsby operation, servicing many prestigious customers, including the art department of De Montfort University, and housing the extensive framing works where timeless skills still underpin the company's commercial success.

A second shop opened at 22 Market Place, in 1913 and a third in 1925 which operated for many years at 104 London Road. The business was flourishing. But it was in the 1930s that the company really began to spread its wings - when the Gadsby offspring were all eager to make their own active contribution. It was a time of desperate straits for many old established picture

framers and gilders - a huge number were going out of business - but Frank Gadsby saw what the circumstances demanded: modernisation, diversification and, crucially, a centralised workshop whose output could be sold through a network of specialised outlets across the country.

In 1927, Frank's son John moved to Walsall to take over the shop of a gilding and framing business his father had bought from a Mr Lamb. Mr Brummit's carving and gilding concern in Lincoln was taken over in 1935: its priceless wood moulds and other tools and equipment were brought to Braunstone Gate, and its premises opened as a shop in 1936 under George (another son) Gadsby's watchful eye. In 1938 a sixth branch came into being when Gadsby's acquired a wonderful framing works in New Briggate, Leeds. Shops in Wakefield and Sheffield followed so that by the time of the outbreak of the Second World War the Gadsby name was already widely known and respected.

After the war, a magnificent opportunity presented itself in the form of Bryce Smith's in Hampstead Road, London. Gadsby's took it over and established a new operation, manufacturing artists' materials. The Market Place branch in Leicester was already a successful provider of artists' materials for Midlands customers, but London offered unique access to discerning, and much larger markets.

Hand in hand with commercial considerations has been a commitment to the highest standards of craftsmanship. Frank's pre-eminence in the world of Fine Art earned him the role of Master of the Fine Art Trade Guild in the 1930s, and an enduring dedication to

unrivalled quality led to his son Bill receiving the same accolade for three years in the 1970s.

Third and fourth generations of the family are now actively involved in the firm, providing a continuity matched only by an unwavering reputation for excellence. Together, they have carved for the company an unparalleled niche in the aesthetic life of the nation.

Above: The shop at 22 Market Place, Leicester in 1935.
Below: Staff from the early days, if only they could see what the business is like today, what would they think?

For hearth and home

J S Millington & Sons Ltd, the countrywide builders merchants, began life at the height of the Victorian era supplying that most 19th century of commodities - coal.

John Smith Millington started out as an engine driver on our nation's early railways. In those heady days of steam who could fail to be impressed by the immense power generated by a steady flow of coal? But when he came to form his own business, John Millington turned his attention to the domestic market. It was in 1860, that he set up as a coal merchant - at a depot in William Street, Leicester. A one-man band at the start, he hired out handcarts to customers, who collected fuel stocks themselves from the yard. The idea was simple, and effective, and before long there was an abundance of customers.

In time, John was able to invest in horses and drays and provide deliveries himself - an easier task once his son, another J S Millington, joined him in the

business. Millington's coal carts became a common - and welcome - sight around the town and, although lorries were introduced even before the First World War, horses continued to play a vital role until much later. Indeed Rod Millington, currently at the helm of the business - and the great great grandson of its founder - has a charming boyhood memory to prove it. He recalls that, as a very young lad, he was once in the office with his father when an enormous clattering of hooves suddenly broke the afternoon air - a horse and cart evidently arriving at great speed. They went outside to investigate and were surprised to find a dray being pulled into the side entrance without a sign of a driver! The mystery was soon solved, however - the dray had taken a delivery of coal to a pub in Birstall, some three miles away, and in time-honoured fashion the driver and loader had been offered a drink 'on the house' for their trouble. The 'drink' soon turned into a bucket of beer, and now driver and loader were both sound asleep on the back of the cart - the trusty old mare had made her own way home!

In 1913, the business acquired its current premises in Humberstone Road and continued to trade

Above: Centred is the founder J S Millington, left and right is A Millington and J M Millington the sons of the founder.
Left: Pre-war, Millington's Luton Depot.

exclusively as a coal and forage merchant for some twenty years. By this time, J S (the younger) had two sons, Arthur, and J M Millington, both active at the yard and a family tradition was firmly established. It was in 1933, after the arrival in the business of J J Millington (son of J M), that major change was to occur and the firm began for the first time to operate as builders' merchants. This branch of activity was so successful that within four years Millington's was able to expand its operation to Luton and Kettering. Coal trading continued meanwhile and proved a godsend when war broke out in 1939 and disrupted all building work.

Soon after the end of the war - as Britain set about repairing its towns and cities, and massive investment became available for new construction - the builders' merchant side of the business once again took off, but there were other areas of interest too. It was at this time that Millington's started trading as oil

Top: An early coal truck.
Above right: A pre-war view of the Kettering depot.
Above left: A Morris B.M.C transporting Millington's building material in 1957.
Right: Millington's today a thriving company.

distributors and - more significantly - as travel agents. The travel agency operation has proved a dynamic development for the firm. Its inception coincided with a healthy public appetite for more ambitious family holidays, and the explosion in cheaper air travel in the 1960s transformed consumer habits. Nowadays, when we think nothing of people holidaying in Australia or California, it's easy to forget that only forty years ago a fortnight in Spain would have been considered rather exotic!

But it's as builders' merchants that Millington's name is still best known and which a sixth generation of the family now proudly oversees. Coal distribution ceased in the late 1970s and oil in the 1980s. In 1985 the company expanded still further when it acquired a depot in Sutton Coalfield. From its beginnings in Leicester the business now has a national reputation, born of time-honoured values: the customer always comes first and deserves the highest quality service, and the best available price.

A future founded on steady, organic growth in all its enterprises seems certain to ensure for J S Millington & Son a very special place in Leicester's history.

A family affair

Saunders of Stapleton was founded in 1963 by Gerald and Vera Saunders when they decided to run their own business. Thirty five years ago they bought their first lorry by hire purchase through the British Wagon Company Ltd and sub-contracted as hauliers to Bardon Hill Quarries. They lived in Dadlington, near Nuneaton, until the time when their initial investment had grown, in five years, to a small fleet of seven vehicles which was causing them parking problems. They were then carrying coal and scrap metal in addition to quarry stone.

Fortunately the roadside service station just outside Stapleton, with sufficient land to cater for their pressing and future needs, came on the market. As well respected local borrowers they were able to finance the purchase of premises and good will in order to branch out. Mrs. Saunders took over the petrol pump side of the business, and, with the acumen and hard graft which are the hall marks of this successful family business, turned them into a profitable part of the growing company.

Mr. Saunders continued to expand the haulage enterprise as their sons worked their way through school.

Today Mark, Ian and Mick Saunders play important parts in the various enterprises located behind the petrol station forecourt. So well does the family work together as a management team that the parents confidently look forward to handing over, stage by stage, more of the running of the business to their capable offspring until they retire.

The Saunders fleet now comprises twenty vehicles ranging from three and a half tonners, once the basic workhorses of military and civil haulage, to thirty-eight tonners. These vehicles are still sub-contracted to local quarries and companies requiring bulk transport. Their main market is the domestic haulage industry and 'own account' delivery companies which depend on the reliable back up offered by the Saunders' in-house service station.

This enterprise maintains their company fleet and cares for private cars brought in by owners requiring first class servicing by mechanics working for a firm with a reputation to uphold. The MoT testing station is all part and parcel of the normal package provided by many local garages.

Above: An aerial view of Saunders of Stapleton taken in 1969.
Left: A hire purchase agreement from The British Wagon Co Ltd in 1963 for Gerald Clifford Saunders who was a haulage contractor.

The fourth element of the Saunders business is much better known nationally in the commercial vehicles field than it is to the average man in the streets of Leicester. Hidden behind the forecourt buildings is the body building workshop which is probably the Saunder's family's most successful enterprise. Here work the experts that turn plans into three dimensional tailor-made reality. Saunders are well located to cater for a wide range of customers from as far afield as Scotland and the South Coast of England.

Their two hundred or so clients a year are attracted to Saunders of Stapleton by word of mouth recommendation from satisfied customers and commercial vehicle architects. There is no doubt that a well run family firm with a loyal work force of dedicated craftsmen has the edge on larger concerns when it comes to providing top quality in everything they do. Buyers looking for first class materials and

sound workable designs produced to a competitive price find that distance is no obstacle when ordering commercial vehicle bodies from the Saunders workshop. Whatever size, shape and internal fittings a transport company may need they can be sure of friendly helpful service by the Saunders team.

Leadership, at any level, starts at the top where final responsibility always rests. No doubt Gerald Saunders, when a National Serviceman in the Korean War, saw leadership qualities and examples tested to the very limits in that demanding conflict. It is this quality emanating from the family which enables the firm to compete successfully with larger organisations such as Boalloy Bodies in offering a totally personalised service.

The parents ambition is for their three sons to continue to run and expand their parent's business by working together as a family following in the footsteps marked out by Gerald's and Vera's efforts and determination to succeed. To quote Gerald; "We've pulled together and run this business as one big family, including the staff, for thirty-five years and it looks like we'll continue to do so in the future."

Above: A French vintage vehicle using a petrol pump at the Saunders of Stapleton station.
Below: A modern aerial view of Saunders of Stapletons' premises as it is today.

The right foot forward

The well established firm of Equity shoes Ltd was started in 1886 by striking shoe factory operatives in a state of revolt against the unequal share-out of profits. Some of the leading spirits, inspired by reading of a co-operative stove factory in France, felt this was the way forward. Sixty people met in St Margaret's Coffee House on the 16th September 1886 to form the Leicester Boot and Shoe Manufacturing Society Ltd. They later met at the Leicester Co-op to draw plans dependant on collecting weekly subscriptions of from a tanner (6d or 2.5p) to a shilling (1/- or 5p) from fellow strikers with which to finance a new factory. With very little more than £96 in the bank with which to compete against established firms this was courage and faith of a very high order.

They decided to concentrate their limited resources on making women's and girl's shoes. The founders proceeded cautiously as they could not afford any initial failure. In the spring of 1887 some twenty one people started in rented premises in Friars Causeway where much of their capital had been spent on plant and materials. They were determined to make good quality shoes rather than

lower quality. The first year was celebrated with a tea dance in the Albert Coffee house.

The young Equity Works received fulsome plaudits, from the Boot and Shoe Trades Journal, for the quality of design and workmanship in the shoes displayed at the 1888 Crystal Palace Festival. Other trade journals, which had previously decried the concept of operatives running a business, complimented the Society on its management.

After a short period in leased premises, the trade had grown sufficient to justify the Society deciding to build its own factory. With great excitement the premises were occupied in January 1895. All production is still made in those same premises - 42 Western Road, Leicester.

Above: A room full of women working in the closing room.
Left: The original premises in 1886 where the company was formerly named Leicester Co-operative Boot and Shoe Manufacturing Society Limited.
Below: I wonder how old the little boy in the picture is? How times have changed since then. This was the lasting room in the 1920s.

the company name to Equity Shoes Ltd, and eventually in 1964 the Grace Road works was sold. Before the days of TV many workers joined company sponsored sporting and social clubs while long service employees were rewarded with longer holidays. Other signs of the times were the provision of car parking under the new Western Road warehouse for an increas-

This rapid expansion came at a time when burgeoning prosperity among the lower middle classes of literate clerks led to the development of good ready made footwear and clothing products. The wealthy patronised bespoke boot and shoe makers while farm workers still bought their annual pair of hand made boots from village bootmakers until these gave way to cheaper factory products.

The two World Wars brought enormous expansion with military contracts for millions of boots. The 1920s saw the need for painful retraction as men's boots were dropped and even the secure market for ladies shoes came to a halt during the General Strike of 1926. Following this monetary reserves were invested in the latest machinery which paid off in the boom years of the thirties, forties and fifties. The company's Golden Jubilee in 1936 was celebrated in style with a splendid tea dance, concert and whist drive at the De Montfort Hall in Leicester. In 1940 new contracts dictated the purchase of a new factory. To everyone's surprise they acquired, for £10,000, a fully equipped up to date shoe factory in Grace Road.

The post war period was beset with wartime problems of shortages of labour and materials. The working week was gradually reduced, as was

ingly mobile workforce. As from the beginning all workers are shareholders in the company and, as such, share profits which arise from sound management and shop floor involvement. Outside influences, like the 'three day' week and subsequent miners' strikes affecting power supplies, had less beneficial effects. These were overcome by the marvellous response of all working shareholders working to maintain faith with the courageous founders who built upon a dream a century ago.

Above: The Crystal Palace exhibition where the Leicester Co-operative Boot & Shoe Manufacturing Society Stand was one of the best, dating from 1923.
Below: The lasting room in 1986.

Constructive creativity and craftsmanship

Norman & Underwood are the oldest and largest cast lead roofing company in the United Kingdom. The company was established in 1825 when brothers in law and plumbers, Thomas Norman and John Underwood formed a partnership.

At first their work consisted of general plumbing, domestic and commercial glazing, decorating and some building. Their premises were in Free School Lane, Leicester, from where the business is still run today. In those days it consisted of a small cottage which was also used as a residence. Goods were delivered by horse and dray and lead was melted by using charcoal.

Lack of capital meant that expansion was slow to begin with but adjacent land was acquired at the present site, as it became available and as it could be afforded. Where land was not available, sites were later purchased at King's Lynn, Corby and Leeds.

Norman & Underwood is a service industry and so, during both the first and second World Wars activities and personnel were reduced to skeletal proportions. However, the company managed to survive in spite of a severe shortage of both materials and labour.

The lead is still cast on open sand beds in a process which has changed little since Roman times. It ensures even thickness and high quality resulting in the longest possible life.

In 1971 the company introduced stainless steel roofing into Britain and has since completed work on several major projects, notably the award-winning Swan Theatre at Stratford.

Norman & Underwood's work in copper, zinc and aluminium has also been a feature of many projects in such places as Leicester Cathedral, the Derby Civic Centre and Loughborough University.

The company has recast and relaid many roofs on York Minster, the most important one being the relaying of the fire damaged South Transept. Other work has included recasting and relaying three of the main tower roofs of Caernarvon Castle, similar work on the roofs of Chatsworth House, Selby Abbey and Westminster Abbey.

Above and left: The founders Thomas Norman and John Underwood.
Below: A view of experienced craftmanship burning a motif onto a cast lead rainwater head.

Norman & Underwood clad the Dome of St Paul's Cathedral in 1968 in lead, which was another work of art that they achieved, and also the Main Nave Roof in 1981.

Contracts from abroad are taken on as and when the company's quotations are found acceptable. Work taken on in the recent past has included cladding the Dome of the Rock in Jerusalem in gold plated bronze, whereby at the present time they are expecting to install the copper roof at the new embassy in Moscow.

Glazing contracts have included leaded light stained glass windows for Japan, Pakistan and the Gulf States. Specialist glazing work has been done in Beirut and the Lebanon.

Today, that small partnership of 1825 has grown into a group employing more than 240 people at a 2-acre site in Leicester, together with a 4-acre facility at King's Lynn in Norfolk. Currently the company comprises three divisions, Glass, Roofing and Plumbing Supplies.

With the fourth and fifth generation of the Underwood family actively participating in the Group's affairs, it is the policy to offer a service and craft second to none in meeting customers' requirements at competitive prices. The Group is a leading member of all the reputable trade associations affiliated to their industry.

Norman & Underwood's business philosophy is to offer the best quality, give a reliable service and charge a competitive price. Specialist skills are offered by a trained personnel. The company works with kite-marked glass and roofing products and holds ISO 9002 assurance.

Company plans for the future are to further improve its reputation and to expand despite continual obstacles in the construction industry.

Above: The York Minster with its re-cast and re-laid roofs, which was one of many minsters and cathedrals that Norman and Underwood superbly repaired with its expert craftmanship.
Left: An aerial view of one of the company's divisions.

Spinning yarns

Worsted spinning and wool stapling were for centuries of central importance to Leicester's prosperity, but in recent times have all but disappeared from the area. With them have passed a multitude of old skills and stories. Or very nearly. The company of Donisthorpe & Co Ltd is a rare survivor from those worsted spinning days with an intricately woven history that vividly depicts the development of mechanised yarn production since the mid-19th century.

The origins of the firm 'Messrs Donisthorpe' are obscure. Tradition has it that the firm was involved in worsted spinning as early as 1739 - but the earliest surviving record is of Alfred Russell Donisthorpe who was spinning at Friars Mill, on the banks of the River Soar, in 1866. Alfred's father, Frederick Donisthorpe, was a dyer and trimmer and it was through a loan to his son that the mill - built probably in the 16th century as a dwelling house - came into family ownership.

The principal market for worsted yarn at this time was Leicester's thriving hosiery industry. Framework knitting had undergone a protracted mechanisation process, dogged by political unrest, but by 1850 the

industry was increasingly being conducted in new factories, whose abundant capacities generated a healthy demand for worsted thread. Alfred diversified his business into other areas too. Contemporary trade directories list a number of companies operating from the mill including, in 1877, A Donisthorpe & Nephew (described as wool combers, wool staplers, merchants and brokers) and F Donisthorpe & Son (wool spinners).

By all accounts, Alfred Russell Donisthorpe was a colourful fellow. It is reported that he possessed only two patterns of day suit - either black-and-white check or brown-and-white check - and that when ordering from his tailor would memorably insist 'the left leg must be turned up and the right leg turned down'. At the height of his career he was a very wealthy man and took great pleasure in a lavish lifestyle (always in rented properties). His shooting parties at Coleorton Hall, near Ashby-de-la-Zouch, were legendary and he was in the habit of ordering wine from London at the rate of ten dozen bottles a time. Nothing pleased him more than emulating the life of landed gentry, and, happily, with his undoubted success in business, he was able to afford it.

When he died in 1906, the family business was floated as a limited liability company and his son, Frederick Russell Donisthorpe took over as Managing Director and Chairman.

Frederick Russell had inherited his father's enthusiasm for social diversion and his education at Rugby School and later Hamburg University prepared him little for

Above left: Frederick Russell Donisthorpe, 1864-1948.
Above right: Frederick Ellis, wool stapler. Alfred Donisthorpe was his best customer.
Left: Staff hard at work in the roving room at Friars Mill in 1922.

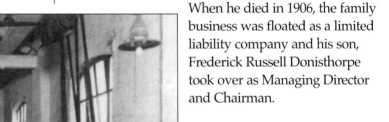

knitting became the firm's chief concerns, until a transformation in 1962, in the form of a mystery thread. A chance encounter led to Donisthorpe acquiring sole selling rights in the UK and Europe for a revolutionary product: an 'extruded' filament of nylon, unlike other sewing thread, which required no spinning and doubling. Soft, flexible and translucent, no dyeing was necessary, for it simply assumed the colour of the surrounding fabric. Eventually, 'monofilament' (as it is called) production started at Friars Mill, later successfully relocating to a purpose-built factory in Craven Street and subsequently to larger premises in Canning Place.

business life. Company decisions fell increasingly to George Ernest Ellis, who had joined the firm in 1889 at the age of 14 and became a director in 1907 (eventually taking over as MD in 1937). The business over which they presided was equipped with both lambswool and worsted spinning machinery, operated in the machine knittings and shoddy trade, and was engaged in dyeing both 'in the wool' and as yarn. Production of yarn was the principal process but there was also some involvement in alpaca and mohair, and woven hair - destined for the German toy doll industry - was also manufactured.

In 1921, Donisthorpe acquired W M Storey's business in York Road. This was an important departure for the firm since it allowed diversification (into sewing cotton) just as other worsted spinners were beginning a period of decline. On the wool side, by the 1930s the company had become exclusively suppliers to wholesalers of machine knittings and mendings, etc., with a single valued retail customer in the form of F W Woolworth.

The Second World War wrought many horrors in Leicester - but, miraculously, the mill survived unscathed. Wool rationing followed and caused the firm real problems. Soon it was clear that new markets must be found, and new products. When George Ellis died in 1948, his son, Shirley, took over - and a modern era of remarkable change began.

Synthetic fibres were already making serious inroads into the traditional industries supplied by Donisthorpe. Dyeing, sewing threads and hand

Donisthorpe of today is a far cry from its 18th century origins. Since 1988, it has been part of the French textile group DMC and has prospered to become the second largest sewing thread manufacturer in the UK. The company has maintained its history of diversification and is now also a distributor of products such as linings and zip fasteners, meeting the changing needs of its customers.

Above: Donisthorpe's mill on the Soar, unchanged after 200 years - a mill that's built to last. How many faces have those walls seen?
Below: Former Board Members of Donisthorpe. From left to right are Alex Reid, Barry Butler and Eric Trevor-Roper with Managing Director Howard Ellis seated (son of Shirley Ellis).

Trips and treks and travel for all

In 1961, Leon Page and Tony Moy were working together in Leicester and discovered a mutual passion in motor racing. The annual 24 hour race in Le Mans was a favourite destination for all enthusiasts, and Leon and Tony set about organising a group trip to the event, handling all travel and accommodation requirements themselves. A party of 23 were fulsome in their praise for the duo's splendid initiative and efficiency, and the venture was repeated in the Summer of 1962. Word had spread by now and the party swelled to 280. It was a stunning success, and in November of the same year Page & Moy, the company, was established.

Now the business was on a firm footing it could move from Leon's home in Silverdale Drive, Thurmaston to its own office space in New Walk. Josephine Allen, a long-time colleague of both Tony and Leon, immediately joined the new Company and has remained there ever since. Today, she manages the firm's mailing requirements; in the early days, every member of the small team happily turned their hand to anything and everything.

1963 - the Company's first serious year of operation - saw an extensive programme of tours to Formula One Grand Prix motor races throughout the world. The swinging sixties

proved to be a perfect setting for the fledgling enterprise - epitomised as they were by a thirst for glamour and excitement after the long austerity of the fifties, and fizzing with new opportunities for travel and adventure. Furthermore, this early concentration on motor racing brought Page & Moy into contact with senior personnel in the motor manufacturing industry who were to become important and long-lasting clients.

Page & Moy's motor racing packages provided a perfect hospitality tool for manufacturers to reward hard-working staff, and to entertain valued clients and other VIPs. The Company was quick to see the attractions of this new market and became an early provider of corporate group travel to all corners of the globe on behalf of a burgeoning range of 'Blue Chip' organisations. As the efficacy of hospitality provision developed alongside a host of other marketing and 'motivational' strategies, Page & Moy found they were increasingly asked to offer more than simply

Above: John Elsom, the current chairman of the company with the late Diana Dors at the London Offices.
Left: Leon Page and Tony Moy at work in the 1970s.

travel organisation and expertise. In 1975, an entirely new operation was set up to concentrate on this sphere of activity. Known first as the 'Conference Division' and later as the 'Motivation Division' it soon garnered for the Company an enviable reputation for dynamic thinking and effectiveness. By 1985, the Division was installed in Brocket Hall, Hertfordshire - but soon outgrew its premises. In 1987, the Division relocated to a three-storey building in Rickmansworth, but when this area of the business continued to expand at a furious rate, it was eventually incorporated into a separate company - devoted to all aspects of motivation, corporate and incentive travel, and associated marketing services - known as Page & Moy (Marketing) Ltd and based in Milton Keynes.

There has been commensurate success in other areas of the business too. The travel industry as a whole was developing rapidly in the early to mid-sixties, but Page & Moy always found scope for innovative ideas of their own. They reasoned that if motor racing had proved successful then it was likely that other sports might offer similar opportunities. The editors of a cycling magazine were soon persuaded of the merits of offering a promotional sports trip to their readers - and when the venture proved more than popular, Page & Moy approached another publication - from the same stable as the cycling magazine, but infinitely better known - Woman's Own. So it was that in April 1968 a trip to the bulb fields of Holland marked the launch of a supremely successful business concept. Look within the pages of your Sunday newspaper, the Radio Times or a myriad other publications today and you will find its thriving modern offspring: the magazine branded readers' holiday offer.

Above: In the very early 1960s the company was known as Page Tours and at that time they only offered motor racing holidays, the picture above is an example of one of their early promotions.

Below: This story is presented in an early 1970s internal newspaper, which informed staff of company progress and success.

Page & Moy rescue a 25 year old tradition at the eleventh hour

With the main exception of the war years the Isle of Man has been top of the pops for Motor Cycle enthusiasts from every corner of the globe who visit the T.T. races every June.

For 25 years or so, there has been an annual pilgrimage by hundreds of U.K. fans for the high spot of the week's activities and the mountain races for the large 150 mph+ bikes run on the Friday.

The complete arrangements had been handled on behalf of the "Motor Cycle" paper by another travel concern. Early in 1974 our Marketing Executive David Short was called by a very worried representative of "Motor Cycle" with the news that there were no plans for the day visit in June and the whole trip looked in jeopardy for 1974.

Undaunted, David Short reviewed and changed the entire arrangements used in previous years, organised a fleet of coaches from all over the U.K. and ended up taking 700 excited fans to the Isle of Man.

With time on his side, David Short has extended the arrangements this year with a coach network covering no less than 51 towns in England, Scotland and Wales.

It should be pointed out that the three day trip, costing about £10 is only for the most hardy!

In 1974 the boat from Liverpool completed the 72 mile crossing of the Irish Sea to Douglas in a gale which had *moderated* to force 8. The weather improved very quickly and provided an exciting day's sport for the fans who already had one uncomfortable and sleepless night under their belts. By the time they reached Liverpool on the overnight crossing, torrential rain had set in and the choppy sea prevented sleep for the second night.

Ready for any contingency, fans were saved from a soaking by 21 waiting coaches only 50 yards from the quayside.

Race fans were quickly transferred and only twenty minutes after docking, the coaches were speeding their tired, but happy, passengers to homes all over the U.K. in time for breakfast.

Page & Moy meet the needs of Exhibition visitors

European exhibitions are attracting more and more visitors from Britain. Businessmen are realising that trade fairs present an opportunity to become aware of the latest developments in their particular industry.

But travel is expensive and many companies cannot justify the very high cost of sending executives to an exhibition when flight and hotel bills could add up to over £200. It was this fact that interested Page & Moy.

By using charter aircraft Page & Moy found that they could offer a full day at an exhibition, including coach transfers and entrance tickets, in some cases for less than half the scheduled air fare. Furthermore departures from Luton meant easy access from most parts of the country. These day flights promoted through trade magazines and associations have for many become the accepted way of visiting important European trade fairs. At an inclusive cost of around £38 a trip to Frankfurt is excellent value — the scheduled air fare alone is over £80.

In 1975 over 3000 businessmen will travel with Page & Moy in this way, between them visiting 30 trade fairs. This is another part of Page & Moy's service to industry and commerce.

horticulture, classical history, architecture...) are separately, and impressively, nurtured - whilst, since 1994, a working association with the National Trust has seen a flourishing expansion in British-based cultural trips.

For many years, Page & Moy steered clear of travel retailing, not only as a retailer itself but also by avoiding travel agents altogether for the sale of their holidays. In many respects, this was consistent with the Company's origins as a supplier of specialised products designed to meet the specific requirements of known customers. Direct selling fulfiled these objectives adeptly. On the other hand, the Company's characteristic flood of ideas was by the mid-1970s already yielding imaginative solutions for what Tony and Leon perceived as endemic shortcomings within the established retail trade. But their efforts, at this time, stalled in the face of a welter of restrictive practices within the industry, coupled with a defensive intransigence on the part of its leaders. It was a brick wall which took some years to erode - and not until the mid-1980s were Page & Moy able to

In 1979, meanwhile, Page & Moy moved into their own branded direct sales brochure. Designed for a growing list of enthusiastic customers, and an already extensive database of potential new clients, the first Special Selection brochure was produced which in subsequent years has blossomed into the Holiday Collection and Cruise Collection brochures. Page & Moy holidays are characterised by an emphasis on revealing the unique spirit and culture of all destinations, through carefully designed itineraries, judicious choice of accommodation, and the presence of expert tour guides skilled at uncovering the treasures of destinations as varied as Renaissance Italy, the Blue Danube, the Highlands of China, even the Perfume River in Vietnam!

The Company's expertise in catering for holidaymakers hungry for more than simply sun and sand has also led to the development of their Cultural Tours. Special interests (in, say, opera,

Above: Spreading the news about an exhibition that was set for over 3000 businessmen to see.
Below left: One of many modern leaflets and brochures the company presents today to customers.
Below: The head office in the 1970s which is still growing and getting better.

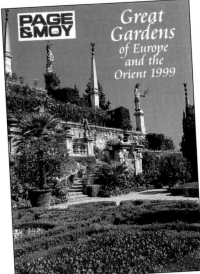

capitalise on a genuinely welcoming climate. Nonetheless, in 1980 there was sufficient passing trade at the Company's main location in Leicester to persuade them to embark on retailing. When the endeavour proved not only straightforward but lucrative a second, and more conventional, shop was opened in the heart of Leicester in 1982. It quickly established itself as one of the city's leading travel agencies and was eventually sold in 1988.

What Page & Moy were able to bring to travel retailing was fresh energy and innovative techniques born out of their extensive background and expertise in direct selling, combined with high levels of customer-awareness. Some tour operators didn't like it, but with the support of a few other like-minded retailers and the eventual involvement of the Monopolies and Mergers Commission, it was soon clear that restrictive practices were doomed. Page & Moy got on with the job of looking after their customers.

In 1986, just as the final vestiges of the old ways were passing into history, Page & Moy helped launch the Barclaycard Holiday Club. A similar incentive scheme had already proved profitable with Walkers Crisps in 1983 - but the runaway success of the Barclaycard project surpassed all expectations. Additional staff were rapidly recruited, but it was soon clear that more sophisticated technology and a great deal more space were going to be essential. Other companies - including TSB, Yorkshire Bank and the Woolwich Building Society - were soon beating a path to Page & Moy's door, eager to establish their own corporate holiday clubs. Barclaycard, however, remained the company's largest client - and discerned in Page & Moy a perfect arena in which to develop their own travel interests. In June 1988, Barclays plc purchased 100% of the company's shares.

Expansion meanwhile continued apace - premises purpose-built at 136-138 London Road in 1973 were soon enlarged by the addition of the building next door, and in 1986 the company took over the first floor of 132-134 London Road. The Holiday Offers Department at the same time found a home of its own in Abbey House. The company demonstrated a characteristically innovative approach to the application of computer technology and was one of the first companies in the UK to use fourth generation language - a decision which helped guarantee that by 1987 Page & Moy had become the largest single retail travel agency outlet in the UK.

At the end of 1993, the executive board of directors acquired a controlling interest via a Management Buyout. The enterprise and vision of the two founders remain, however, as defining qualities in Page & Moy's remarkable success - and a company ethos that puts people squarely at the centre of every decision augurs well for a dynamic role in the new Millennium.

Above: Fantastically designed brochures for the modern Page & Moy which is here to stay.

A cut above the rest

The origins of the present company, T S Bloor & Sons Ltd can be traced back to a pork butchery business established in the early 1890s by Mr A Bloor, great-grandfather of the present MD Mr Charles Bloor, and father of Mr T S Bloor whose name still graces the operation of the firm today. Tom learned his craft under the expert supervision of his father at his business in Melton Road, Leicester before joining the army to fight in the First World War.

In 1927, he set up his own business as a manufacturing pork butcher, from premises in Coalville, Leicestershire. In those early days he made all his own products using traditional tools and belt-driven equipment.

Before long, the business was doing so well that he was able to move to a larger retail shop and extend his operation by obtaining facilities to produce pork pies, sausages and cooked meats. By 1937 Mr Bloor was in a position to buy land on which he built an abattoir, together with a cutting plant and curing facility. It was in the early 1950s that this site was transformed into the mighty Belvoir Bacon Company Ltd, which, within a few years, employed a workforce of around 300, supplying hams, pies and other products for wholesale distribution throughout the UK.

Above: T.S. Bloor, in the late 1950s.
Inset: T.S. Bloor outside the shop in 1927, with the window displaying fresh meat that has helped the business to prosper.
Below: The original shop in Melton Road, the little boy is T.S. Bloor at the turn of the century.

The years of the Second World War brought rationing and a shortage of labour, but the firm went to enormous lengths to keep customers supplied with high quality products as before, and made every effort to maintain the standards they had set themselves in spite of all difficulties.

Mr Bloor had his own philosophy and a set of maxims which his staff, and he himself had to live up to. He made a point of never asking a member of staff to do anything he either could not or would not do himself. No-one in the firm was allowed to turn out a product that they would not happily eat themselves - every product had to be of the highest quality and offered for sale at a fair price. Mr Bloor's motto was always 'Keep it simple!'.

The company was incorporated in the sixties and continued to be known for its reliability, integrity and consistency. Mr Bloor always kept in close communication with both his staff and his customers. This 'hands on' approach to leadership ensured that the business has maintained the highest standards throughout its history. Today, the management listens to the workforce and to its customers so that wants are readily anticipated and misunderstandings avoided.

In April 1995 a new factory, under the T S Bloor name, was purpose-built in Coalville. Here, with the enterprising control of Charles Bloor, state-of-the-art machinery now processes prime legs of pork into high quality cooked hams.

Having built up an enviable reputation for quality over the years. The company plans to maintain the high standards which it has set for itself.

The company aims to achieve the EFSIS accreditation by the end of 1998 to enable it to move forward in the market place and to move forward into the millennium. The company looks set to hold expansion into consumer packs popular slice market.

T S Bloor continues to hold its head up against stiff competition from other manufacturers of cooked hams in the EEC.

Above: Charles Bloor.
Left: David and T.E Bloor twenty years ago.
Below: The new shop on the day it opened in 1978 in Coalville.

An experimental rubber bollard situated at the junction of Charles Street and Belgrave Gate in 1933.

ACKNOWLEDGMENTS

THE PUBLISHERS WOULD LIKE TO THANK

LILY HICKMAN

LEICESTERSHIRE MUSEUMS ARTS & RECORDS SERVICE:
LEICESTERSHIRE RECORD OFFICE

DEREK STONES

FAMOUS IN THEIR FIELD

FRED WHOWELL OF HAWKSHAW

Fred Whowell

There is more than one way to get to Bolton from Bury, but perhaps the most pleasant is to take the single-decker bus via Tottington, Greenmount and Hawkshaw. As the bus approaches Holcombe Hill one may think it is going to climb the heights, but suddenly it turns left into a rural route as pleasant as the hill itself and beyond the little cottages and a few more dwellings of Hawkshaw, you can see a wide stretch of countryside and undulating woodland.

The village of Hawkshaw intrigues me. I can imagine long-dead tenants of the little cottages refreshing themselves in the two ancient hostelries and see the bright, cheerful faces of the early followers of John Wesley in the late 18th century. The present church is the second one, and before its predecessor was built they had the school, already operating by 1803.

The rugged chimney of Bleaklow Mill once emitted smoke produced during the cotton spinning process. Established in 1834 by Rigg Brothers Ltd, it carried on trading as such for well over a hundred years. The old mill is now used by the Woodhey Dyeing Company.

The locality was well-timbered with oak trees and no doubt the name 'Hawkshaw' is a corruption of 'oak' and 'shaw' (a small wood or thicket). The famous 'old oak' at the entrance to the village was celebrated a hundred years ago in the sign of an adjacent wayside inn: 'Let the Old Oak Stand'. Incidentally, I was nearly born just across the road. My parents' first home was a small cottage there, but they moved to Ramsbottom just before I arrived on the scene.

Croich Hey, a pleasant mansion which is now a home for elderly people, has an older name than that of the village itself. It appears in records as early as 1324, variously spelt, and up to 1609 Charles Barlow of Croislawe was lord of the manor. Bury Parish Registers show that by the mid-1600s the district was known as Croichley Fold, after the hamlet of that name, and it was still called so at the time of the 1841 census, when eight families were living there.

The house Croich Hey was built in 1904 by Fred Whowell, then a director of the Bleachers' Association, who lived all his life in the village and consequently knew its ancient history. His father, Charles, moved from Bradshaw in 1850 to take over Two Brooks Mill, a bleaching concern now demolished. Conditions in the mill were not ideal. Even in the 1850s, when Charles was not supervising the mill personally, workers did a minimum fifteen-hour day and complained of aching legs and sore feet. Before Charles Whowell arrived things were worse still, and around 1830 there had been quite a scandal involving the bribery of two excise officers at Two Brooks.

At that time the works was producing printed cloth, on which duty was payable. The excise men had to stamp the cloth and some of the printers got into the habit of plying two officers with free drinks, gifts of salmon and free dresses for their wives. The careers of all concerned came to a sticky end when the excise department found out. Of the employers, one fled to America and the other spent some years in jail at Lancaster Castle. One of the dismissed excise men went to run a pub in Liverpool but died soon afterwards, the other apparently took to the bottle and was killed in an accident as he was riding through Quarlton, drunk in charge of his horse.

Fred Whowell, born in 1855, was the last of Charles's 13 children, who all lived at Higher Brook Bottom Farm. When Charles died, Fred conducted the bleaching business with three brothers and in the course of time ran it alone. Around 1900 he was living at Carr Bank, a house built by one of his brothers, and at that time he sold out the business to the Bleachers' Association, joined the board of the latter and became one of its general managers.

In addition to the business commitments which brought him prosperity, Fred Whowell had a

Rigg's Mill (now the Woodhey Dyeing Company) 1989

natural inclination towards agriculture and horticulture and conducted many of his own experiments in this field. Among other things he developed a method of successfully storing hay gathered in a wet state, and he was also keenly interested in the breeding and rearing of pigs in natural, open-air conditions. Men were employed on his Devon estates to look after a thousand or more of these delightful animals.

He visited India to look at cotton factories there, bringing back so many souvenirs that Croich Hey was described as 'a very treasure house of Indian products', and I'm sure the villagers must have been fascinated by his visitor from Delhi in 1912, the Hon Raj Bahadur Lala Sultan Singh.

But above all Fred Whowell had a personality which inspired deep affection among the people around him. He was often referred to as 'The Squire of Hawkshaw' and when he built Croich Hey it became a sort of 'Liberty Hall', whose hospitality many local people got the chance to share. I myself enjoyed a visit about 1920 when, in spite of a wet day, the scout troops of Bury marched up to Croich Hey for tea. There was a verandah full of tables laden with sandwiches, pies, cakes and jugs of tea, Afterwards the rain ceased and we were allowed to play around the grounds.

At the time of the 1926 miners' dispute, Mr Whowell got out the old 17th century maps of his

St Paul's Church, Bury, as it is today

estate at Quarlton to search for old coal pits. He turned over one seam to out-of-work colliers so the men could earn a living and the village of Hawkshaw got its coal at normal prices.

This big-hearted gentleman died

in 1927 and for eighteen years his home and grounds were open to all the old folk of the area for an annual treat. On the day of his funeral every house and shop in the village had its blinds drawn.

LINKS WITH ST PAUL'S

The grave of John Just, second master of Bury Grammar School, can be seen in the extensive churchyard of St Paul's, consecrated in 1842 and only the third church in Bury. Most of the graves have been grassed over but the one in memory of John Just stands up in monumental splendour.

He was born in 1797 near Kendal and when he was about 20 he became interested in antiquarian pursuits and started investigating the Roman roads. His research in field and country gave him the opportunity to find out more about natural history and in the summer months he would rise at four o'clock to pursue what became his favourite study, botany. He settled in Bury, continuing his literary and scientific studies and at the same time taking in private pupils. In 1832 the second mastership of Bury Grammar School became vacant and he was unanimously elected to the post, which he held for the rest of his life. He was appointed lecturer on botany at the Royal Manchester School of Medicine and Surgery a year later and in 1848 was made honorary professor of botany at the Royal Manchester Institution. He died in 1852.

For much of the nineteenth century Bury became a real

Two Brooks mill chimney, the only part of the mill still standing

centre of music and song, and one of the best teachers of the day was John Mellin Wike, who was the organist and choirmaster at St Paul's. The services there were raised to the highest pitch and the many vocalists were well trained. The congregation also appreciated the choirboys' uniformity of dress - they were the first in Bury to wear surplices. Mr Wike was a great friend to the townspeople in general and in the 1860s produced the well known play, 'The Miller and his Men', for charity - at least, he took charge of the music. The histrionics were attended to by Clock Shaw, famous as a painter of Bury scenes and as a friend of Henry Irving, who came from Manchester to assist in another production for which Mr Wike was musical director, 'Hamlet'. Everybody in Bury went to see 'The Miller' and in spite of one or two amateurish shortcomings, it was voted a great success.

At that time Bury had several professional musicians, notably Richard Hacking, one time organist at Bury Parish Church. He went to Oxford, where he took the degree of

Virginia Mill datestone, still in situ

Bachelor of Music in 1855, composing the cantata 'Judgement and Mercies' for his exercise. He presented it to the Bury Town Hall and it was included in the programme for the Christmas concert that year at the recently-built Athenaeum. Sims Reeves sang the tenor part, and with one of the world's greatest singers performing a work by a local composer, I imagine the hall was crammed with an enthusiastic and emotional audience.

A local conductor and violinist was Harry Nuttall, a member of the famous Halle Orchestra for forty years. Charles Halle himself had appeared in Bury in 1856 and said that 'he had enjoyed the evening programme; the people of Bury were very intelligent and appreciative.' When, in 1877, he was not able to appear, Harry Nuttall conducted in his stead.

A promising chorister in his youth, Harry Nuttall had trained under J M Wike at St Paul's and learnt the violin from a relative of another St Paul's organist, Alcimus Coulthurst. He was involved in both 'The Miller and his Men' and 'Hamlet' and in addition to the Halle, he played for the Liverpool Philharmonic and the Huddersfield Choral Society, meeting many famous musicians in the process. He died on 30th April 1927 at the age of 85, survived by twelve of his fourteen children.

For special Sermon days the Bury church choirs would perform oratorios and the custom was to supply a small quantity of tobacco to those

Memorial to Fred and Alice Whowell at Hawkshaw

taking part. In 1859, however, a Sunday school (not necessarily St Paul's) decreed, 'No tobacco to be furnished for the singers.' Whether the choir improved is not recorded, but after three years it was resolved 'that $\frac{1}{4}$lb tobacco be provided for the use of male singers.'

Perhaps they got the tobacco from the works of Thomas Blunt & Sons in York Street. Although this was a cotton waste dealer's in later years, a datestone still bears the legend 'Virginia Mill 1884', revealing an earlier use. It was built by Frederick Smith, who had established a tobacco, snuff and cigar factory in 1864. The site of this early works is unknown, but in 1871 he was in Stanley Street and ten years later he had moved to Bolton Street. Business was obviously flourishing and he decided to name his new works after his high-class product.

Thomas Blunt's works in York Street

BILLINGTON OF BACUP

My father's family came from Bacup and in my young days they were all very proud of 'Billington of Bacup, the world's greatest swimmer'. It was only when I took up local history that I decided to trace his remarkable career.

David Billington was born in Bacup in 1885 and his father was superintendent of the local swimming bath. Naturally the youngster was introduced to water at an early age, and he didn't like it. His father, however, said he had to like it, threw him into the deep end and told him to find his way out!

In spite of this drastic beginning, David Billington became one of the finest swimmers in the world. When he was thirteen he was designated 'Boy Champion of England' and by the time he was nineteen had won nine national championships over distances ranging from 440 yards to one mile. He also won the King Edward VII Cup, awarded for a combination of speed swimming and life saving, and he swam before the King and Queen Alexandra in London. In addition, he was the victor in the famous River Thames 'Lords and Commons Race' over a distance of 5 miles, 60 yards.

That was in 1905, and the same year he competed in one of the greatest continental races of the period, the $7\frac{1}{2}$ mile swim along the River Seine through Paris. Unfortunately the French laws of swimming were different from those of Britain's Amateur Swimming Association and Billington was declared a professional. He appealed to the committee, but after long consideration and even allowing for partial agreement between the two factions, the original decision stood.

So after winning 300 prizes as an amateur Billington was forced to turn professional. In this field he was equally successful, and at one period held every professional championship from 100 yards to $13\frac{1}{2}$ miles. He competed in the Seine race many times and only lost once when he had to retire with cramp.

He came to Bury in 1913 to take part in what was to be one of the greatest swimming contests ever held in the town. Oscar E Dickman, the great Australian swimmer, had challenged him to race for the one mile championship of the world and Billington accepted. The event was promoted by Bury Corporation

and was held on August 2nd at the Clarence Recreation Ground reservoir. It was a magnificent affair, well advertised and about 5,000 1s tickets were sold.

On the appointed day the weather was all that could be desired and over 7,000 people assembled around the reservoir embankment. The referee was H W Keen of the 'Sporting Life'; W H Broome of the Royal Life Saving Society was check-starter and R Grime and G Studholme of the Bury and Elton Swimming Club were the judges. Billington won by 108 yards in the record time of 24 minutes 11 seconds. The event made £105.1.9d, of which the Corporation took 20% for charities; Billington got £50.1.10d and Dickman £33.10.7d. I believe the winner also received a cup worth £100 but who supplied that I don't know.

Afterwards David Billington toured the world and was at one time coach, instructor and manager of the civic baths at Hamilton, Ontario, where his coaching ability produced some world class swimmers. His love of gambling was commensurate with his love of swimming and, as with most gamblers, money was 'easy come, easy go'. His ornamental swimming displays at the Tower Circus in Blackpool, and his daring dives from the end of one of the piers wearing clothing which had been set alight before take-off,

David Billington

were very popular attractions for holidaymakers.

He settled in Radcliffe, where he was the schools' instructor at Whittaker Street Baths, and 700 children attended the baths each week to be taught by him. I once spent a pleasant afternoon with his daughter Adelaide and his grandson, Colin Makinson of Radcliffe, and between them they produced a comprehensive chronicle of photographs, records and anecdotes of this celebrated character.

WORKING FOR GOD

JOHN HARPER

The man who contributed most to Bury's church architecture wasn't a native of the town. However, his cousin William was and perhaps that is why he did so much work here.

John Harper, designer of three Bury churches, was born at Dunkenhalgh, near Blackburn, on 11th November 1809. He began his professional studies under the distinguished architect brothers, Benjamin and Philip Wyatt of London, and later set up a practice of his own in York. As much interested in painting as in architecture, in 1836 he and his friends held an exhibition of pictures which ultimately led to the formation of the Art Society. Among the closest of these friends was William Etty R.A, who painted the portrait of John Harper's

sister the same year. (Etty was a native of York and his statue dominates Exhibition Square in front of the City Art Gallery.)

Among Harper's famous patrons were the Duke of Devonshire, who employed him for a time at Bolton Abbey, and Lord Londesborough, but apart from his work in Bury he is probably best known for the Gothic-style proprietary school at Clifton, York.

Unfortunately his talents were never fully realised. In 1842, while travelling in Italy to study art, Harper caught malaria in Rome. Still in a weak state, he made the voyage to Naples, where he died, aged only 33. Etty's tribute to him was published in the 'Morning Herald': *'Active, zealous and* enterprising... To say that he is an irreparable loss to York is saying too little. I think the loss of John Harper a national loss. His talents were only equalled by the great and good qualities of that heart whose pulsations the Almighty has thought fit to arrest. For myself, I know of no-one scarcely that can supply his place - ever ready at a word to do anything great, good or benevolent, with a feeling for Art and the knowledge of it that falls to the lot of few."

St Marie's, the first Roman Catholic church in Bury, built in 1841/42, is one of Harper's best creations. In the perpendicular style, its remarkable feature is the great ornate lantern tower with buttresses and openwork battlements. Beneath is a narthex, or covered porch, flanked by figures of St Edward and St Wilfrid of York. Above the high altar the sunlight pours through a magnificent stained glass window. This great church was opened on 10th August 1842, two months before

All Saints, Elton; from a 19th century drawing

the death of its talented designer. His cousin William was a generous supporter of St Marie's and in his will, 47 years later, left money to pay the ground rent (£77 per annum) to Lord Derby.

The foundation stone of St Paul's, an earlier Bury church attributed to Harper, was laid on October 3rd 1838 by Lord Stanley (afterwards the 14th Earl of Derby). Tea and buns were provided afterwards for the Sunday School scholars, but the workmen chose to give up their customary dinner and drink in favour of new coats and appeared at the ceremony wearing their new clothes. The church was consecrated on June 29th 1842, but at that date £1,200 was still owed to the builders. Thanks to the generosity of Oliver Ormrod Walker of Chesham and Thomas Openshaw of Pimhole, who split the cost between them, this was soon paid off.

Finally the parish church of All Saints, Elton, with its square clock tower, blind arcading and round-headed windows in the Norman style, is another example of John Harper's versatility. He did not live to see it completed and it was consecrated on 29th June 1843. Indeed, it is unlikely that he saw any of his Bury churches standing. Today, nearly 150 years later, they are still appreciated by their congregations and by those with an interest in the history of architecture.

St Marie's, Bury

John Harper's cousin William deserves a footnote to himself, for he too did much for Bury in his own way. Although he was born in Samlesbury, his mother came from Bury and he received part of his education at Bury Grammar School. He set up in business here as a solicitor in 1836 and the following year became Registrar, a post which he held for fifty-two years until his death. He was also a J.P, a captain in the Bury Volunteer Corps and the last clerk to the Bury Improvement Commissioners. In this capacity he was at least partly responsible for securing better streets, sewerage and water supply for the town and was instrumental in getting both the Bury Waterworks Bill and the Bury and Tottington Railway Bill through Parliament.

William Harper

He was also a lover of the people and wanted laymen to have more say in the management of church affairs and greater religious freedom generally. His writings on these and other subjects caused much bitter controversy within the Methodist movement, and by 1797 he had founded what became the 'Methodist New Connexion', though his followers at the time were known simply as 'Kilhamites'. He then undertook long and tiring journeys from his base in Nottingham with the aim of extending his new organisation and returned home at the end of November 1798, completely exhausted. Despite this, he struggled on with some of his engagements, but less than a month later he was dead, at the early age of 36; perhaps his work was done.

WESLEY AND KILHAM

John Wesley is said to have dated his conversion from the Established Church from 24th May 1738, which I believe is known as Wesley Day. He preached at Bury many times during his career and was at the opening of Pits o'th'Moor Chapel in 1774. Legend has it that people brought bad eggs to pelt him with but a Mrs Hall stood in front of him, determined that they should hit her before the visitor. However, the would-be hecklers were too gallant to pelt a lady and didn't throw their ammunition. Perhaps Wesley didn't notice, for his diary records that the people at 'the new house near Bury', like those at Chowbent, were 'as quiet as lambs'.

Not long afterwards there was a preaching house in Cross Street, and by 1785 one in Clerke Street, the forerunner of the Union Street Chapel, which was built in 1815. Bury Reference Library holds an original letter from Wesley, dated 22nd December 1786, in which he gives 'full and free consent to the sale of our Old Preaching house in Bury, Lancashire'.

His strictures on the first Robert Peel are well known; Wesley had breakfast with him in April 1787 and commented on his wealth, 'A few years ago (he) began with five hundred pounds, and is now supposed to have gained fifty thousand pounds. O, what a miracle if he lose not his own soul!' But a year later he was in happier mood, despite a difficult journey over bad roads: 'We met a lively congregation which made us forget our labour.' As

far as I know this was his last visit; he died on 2nd March 1791.

Wesley was born in 1703 at Epworth in Lincolnshire and 59 years later Alexander Kilham was born in the same village. His parents were Methodists and naturally he followed the same beliefs and eventually joined the Methodist Society. He was only 29 years of age when John Wesley died and became an energetic campaigner for Methodist independence, especially where the right of Methodist preachers to administer the Lord's Supper was challenged by conservatives anxious not to upset the Established Church.

As early as 1797 Bury Kilhamites were holding services in an upper room in Moss Lane (now Moss Street). By 1813 they were building their Methodist New Connexion Church and School on Tentersfield, just off Bury Lane (now Bolton Street), and here they stayed for nearly seventy years, until the transfer to the church and school in Heywood Street. Whether this new venture was a joint effort with another group, or whether the old chapel was worse for wear I have not been able to discover.

I have, however, seen a photograph of a medal struck to commemorate the chapel jubilee. One one side the wording was 'Rev A Kilham Founder of the Methodist New Connexion' and on the other 'Methodist New Connexion Sunday Schools, Bolton Street, Bury. Founded

St Paul's before the graveyard was grassed over

1810. Jubilee 1860. Minister Rev John Weight.' The medals were presented by Mr John Battersby, later to become an alderman and Mayor of Bury in 1901. By then he was an Anglican, but he was connected to the Methodists through his mother, Ellen Smith. His father had been organist at the New Road Congregational Chapel, and music must have played a large part in the Battersby household, for Ellen was the youngest daughter of a very musical New Connexion family; her elder sister was organist at the Bolton Street chapel and her brother a pianist. John Battersby was head of the firm of Robert Battersby & Sons, woollen manufacturers, founded by his grandfather in 1810; their small mill stood in that well known 'little paradise', The Island.

Many senior New Connexion members have recalled the happy Anniversary Sermons preached at Heywood Street and one rather humorous story concerns a Mr Barton, an old preacher from Rochdale who was a frequent visitor to the chapel. He had a dog called Jim Crow which always came with him. Jim, so the tale goes, would stand on his hind legs in the pulpit and join in with the hymn singing – but whether joyfully barking or dolefully howling is not specified!

Shore Fields and the Island before 1900

POINTS NORTH

THE WAY TO HOLCOMBE

Much of the landscape through which the River Irwell flows in its early stages is attractive, and few areas more so than Holcombe, where the hill stands sentinel at the head of Rossendale, its shoulders hunched beneath the memorial tower to Sir Robert Peel which crowns the summit.

Nestling at the foot of the hill, the village of Holcombe Brook was once linked to the communities of Woolfold, Tottington and Greenmount by the railway which was for a brief span the most important feature of the area. Mooted in 1876 as the Bury and Tottington District Railway by a group of local businessmen headed by Joshua Knowles (son of the founder of Tottington printworks), it began operating as a single-track railway in 1882. The Lancashire and Yorkshire Railway took over in 1888; a railmotor service was introduced in 1905 and in 1913 Dick, Kerr & Company installed a high-voltage direct-current, overhead system of electrification at their own cost. This was not just a generous gesture – the firm wanted to carry out experiments with a view to putting in tenders for contracts abroad, but did not want to go to the expense of laying their own track. So they approached

the Lancashire & Yorkshire with their proposals and mutually beneficial arrangements were made. After the first run, the Bury Times reported, 'A speed approaching 50 miles per hour could be obtained, we are informed, but it is not intended at present to accelerate the timetable in operation.'

The line had a comparatively short life for a railway and finally closed in the early 1960s, but much of the route is now available for a pleasant walk past several interesting structures which both delight the eye and arouse curiosity.

The white building, for instance, glimpsed from time to time through the surrounding trees, turns out to be Brandlesholme Hall. With parts said to date from the 13th century, it is wonderfully well preserved and appears to be very much lived in. From the Brandlesholme family, whose name is perpetuated in the nearby road, it passed through marriage to the Greenhalghs. The most prominent member of this family appears to have been Captain John Greenhalgh, who was distinguished as an ardent Royalist during the Civil War and for some years was Governor of the Isle of Man. He fought nobly, I believe, at the Battle

John Battersby, Mayor 1901–02

of Wigan in 1651 and no doubt did the same at the Battles of Bury three years earlier, but unfortunately Oliver Cromwell's lot captured the town. The Roundhead forces, led by Major General Lambert, were entrenched on a bend of the River Irwell near Walmersley, and Major Assheton marched over Cockey Moor and forded the Irwell at Bury Bridge. So attacked on both sides, Bury had no chance. Legend has it that grain grown on the fields of strife near the town was streaked with red, like blood, for more than a century afterwards.

After the Restoration the fortunes of the Greenhalghs revived somewhat. Captain Greenhalgh's son John was made Rector of Bury and another family member, Thomas, was High Sheriff of Lancashire in the 1660s. A century later, however, their star had waned and in 1770 the old Hall was sold off to the Powell family.

The majestic nine-arch Tottington viaduct, which carried the railway over the valley once occupied by Joshua Knowles' calico printworks, may be crossed on foot and few can resist pausing to gaze down from a height of about thirty feet into the waters of the picturesque Island Lodge, where fine specimens of mirror carp may sometimes be seen basking at the surface.

Tower Farm is all that remains of the calico printing empire, a group of mellowed stone buildings topped by a crenellated tower which bears the inscription 'JK 1840'. They were the stables for the horses which hauled the finished merchandise to Manchester and Leeds. The

Brandlesholme Old Hall

John Greenhalgh

story goes that there were Manchester horses and Leeds horses and they were never interchanged, the reason being that they knew the route so well it didn't matter if the driver fell asleep.

GREENMOUNT

Greenmount is not far away and walking towards it along Brandlesholme Road, one may stop to wonder at the origin of a squat tower, half hidden by foliage, standing by the roadside. It bears several irregularly placed, grotesquely carved figures reminiscent of gargoyles, a curiously motley collection of some jocular Greenmount resident of the past.

As one approaches Greenmount along the old railway line, the impressive pile of Hollymount Convent captures the imagination. Gazing benignly down from its elevated position, it has serenely continued a mission of mercy spanning several generations. Built as a private school in 1873, it was taken over in 1888 by the Children's Rescue and Protection Society, following the death of the school's headmaster. At the instigation of the Bishop of Salford, some sisters of a Belgian order of nuns settled there and ran it as a nunnery and orphanage.

There was a brief scandal at the turn of the century when it was claimed that some children were being ill treated, but all was soon well again and Hollymount celebrated its silver jubilee in 1913. By then 40 sisters were running the school

Island Lodge, Tottington and the railway viaduct

with 300 pupils, a nursery, the home and Claremont Secondary School. Sadly, all this space was soon to be needed. Belgian refugees started arriving in 1914 and the following year the sisters were caring for wounded soldiers as well. Classrooms were filled with extra beds to take about 80 men. A similar thing happened during the Spanish Civil War, when 24 Basque children and two teachers, all refugees from the fighting, were accommodated.

Closed as an orphanage in 1961, Hollymount is now devoted to the care of the aged in one part and the education of the young in another.

The Bulls Head at Greenmount is a real mixture of ancient and modern, for a splendid restaurant has arisen at the rear of the old buildings. In 1818 the road from Brandlesholme was just a track called Green Lane and a 'Richard Walkwork' was the proprietor of the Bull Inn at 'Houlkham Lane'. He was still there in 1829 when the spelling was modernised to 'Wallwork' and 'Holcombe', but in 1834 his address was given as 'Lower Tottington'. By 1843 Edward Hopkinson was the boss, and just to add to the confusion, ten years later he was giving his address as 'Nailors Green'. Edward's widow was using the same address as late as 1871, despite the fact that the Bowling Green, a pub contemporary with the Bulls Head and only a short distance down the road, was better known as the Naylors Green Tavern.

Tower Farm, Greenmount

In 1829 this was nearly the scene of a mass murder and one of the victims, James Booth, actually died. The occasion was a dinner for a dozen or so members of the Select Vestry at which the landlord, Mr Kay, had provided meat, vegetables and Hunter's Pudding. Afterwards the whole company were sick and when Mr Booth expired it was discovered that there were traces of white arsenic in the food. A Bury druggist, Joseph Hartley, testified that two men had bought a quantity of the poison from him a few weeks earlier, saying that it was for Mr Kay of the Naylors Green and that they lived there. The landlord stoutly denied all knowledge, protesting that he had kept the house

for more than twenty years and in all that time he had never had poison on the premises. As he and his family had eaten the food and been ill as well, it was concluded that some stranger must have sneaked the poison into the water while the pudding was boiling. Despite the offer of £100 reward for

Children at Hollymount

John Heap, Mayor 1879-80

information leading to a conviction, the culprits were never caught and the motive for the crime remained a mystery.

No ancient buildings are left at the Naylors Green - this pub was pulled down and rebuilt in the 1960s. But the place name goes back to the 17th century and beyond, when everyone was dependent on horses for transport and haulage as well as for farm work and nails were necessary to shoe them. Small workshops sprang up in many villages and the men who specialised in this craft were called nailers. The standard nail was $2\frac{1}{4}$", or one sixteenth of a yard long, and this was later used as a unit of measurement for cloth, which was sold by 'nails' just as horses are measured in 'hands' of 4".

The name Greenmount probably derives from the old Green Lane track and it soon became a desirable place to live. John Heap, a Bury printer who was responsible for publishing the first Bury Times on 7th July 1855, was among those to settle there. He built the church which stands just across from the Bulls Head, and he later became a town councillor and Mayor of Bury.

The old Naylors Green Hotel, 1965

HOLCOMBE

The surrounding area has for many years been associated with hunting and it is not surprising that a number of hostelries have signs representing the sporting fraternity. One of these is the Hare and Hounds Hotel on the main road at Holcombe Brook, the gateway to an extensive tract of country dear to the heart of those who follow the chase.

The eighteenth century Shoulder of Mutton in Holcombe village was in its time associated with both the English Game Fowl Club and the Holcombe Harriers, and when I last visited it, still had a photograph of George V inspecting the Harriers on his visit to Hoghton Tower, near Preston, in 1913. He was not the first monarch to do so, for when James I stayed at Hoghton in 1617 he was so impressed by the Harriers that he decreed they should wear the royal scarlet and gold livery.

The following year, the King was again concerned with the inhabitants of Bury's region. There was a dispute between his agent and the tenants of Tottington, who, it was claimed, had unlawfully improved and enclosed part of the common land, 'unlawfully digg'd up and taken thereout Coal, Slate, Stones, and other Stones, Turves and Peats' and were assuming that they were

Inspecting the Holcombe Harriers at Hoghton Tower, 1913. Left to right: the Huntsman, Major Hardcastle (Master), HM King George V, Lord Derby, Sir J de Hoghton

entitled to fixed rents. They pleaded custom and asked for a settlement and James I decreed in their favour, upon consideration of a sizable sum paid into the royal coffers! His decision was ratified by a similar bill passed in 1641, but unfortunately the Civil War intervened and the good people of Tottington weren't entirely sure of their position until the Restoration.

The grey stone buildings of Holcombe village itself, spilling down the rugged face of the hill and peeping through the leafy lanes and woods of the scattered settlement, recall the placid days of long ago. Hey House, built the year before James I's visit to Lancashire, was at one time used as a hunting lodge by the powerful de Trafford family and the Holcombe Hunt had their first kennels there. Some of the carved woodwork in the house is said to have come from Whalley Abbey. Until the early nineteenth century it was occupied by the Browne family, who were prominent in church affairs. Thomas Browne was an elder of Bury Presbyterian Classis for ten years in the mid-seventeenth century and his descendant, John Holt Browne, a warden of Holcombe Chapel from 1773 to 1776.

Hey House and the Halmot Court House of 1646 are still there, but the old manorial Court House was demolished in 1864, after standing for two hundred years. It is said to have been built by the Duke of Albemarle, to whom Charles II gave lands in Holcombe as a reward for helping him to get his throne

Holcombe Hill and part of the village as seen from the churchyard

back. It was later used as a school and the doorframe, mullioned windows and gargoyles were apparently taken for the construction of School House (or Well House) in Dundee Lane, near School Street, which still bears a triangular lintel with the date 1664 and above, some grotesque figures which could easily have come from an old court of justice. Two four-foot-high stone posts topped with pyramids which once stood at the ends of the jury box were made into gateposts at Holcombe School. I could only find one but a former pupil, Stephen Davenport, remembered

two in his day. The rail connecting them had gone by then - tradition has it that when the old Court House was used as a school, naughty boys and girls were made to sit on this as a punishment. In 1672, Charles II also licensed the Court House to be used for Presbyterian worship, but this was withdrawn a year later when the oppressive Test Act was passed, requiring all office holders to belong to the Church of England.

Holcombe's old chapel was of ancient origin and for many years shared its curate with Edenfield. But it was slightly

Hey House, Holcombe

better off; the 1552 inventory recorded three vestments, a bell, a sacring bell, an old surplice and a brass pax. These were sold for £3.6.8d the following year. The seventeenth century brought hard times for two of the ministers: in 1649 Robert Gilbody was suspended for tippling and being present at a bowling match held on an alehouse green, and in the 1660s Henry Pendlebury was ejected from the living under the Act of Uniformity. By the eighteenth century things were more peaceful and the chapel was enlarged in 1714 and again sixty years later. It was finally demolished in 1851 and a new church built on its site.

Even in the respectable years of the mid-nineteenth century the people of Holcombe had a reputation for being quarrelsome and it was said that many looked forward to a good 'Holcombe Row' at Wakes time. The man who patched up the injured was Dr William Plant Woodcock, whose name was still remembered with gratitude many years after his death. His grandmother was one of the Plants of Plant Farm and the Woodcocks were another old Holcombe family. He was married at Holcombe Old Chapel in 1837 to Eliza Rostron, the daughter of a local gentleman, and when he died in 1884 his name had become a household word to all the villagers, rich and poor alike.

Holcombe Wakes was certainly not an event for weaklings to attend. By 1871 they had moved most of the stalls and side-shows to Ramsbottom, because the fairground people thought Holcombe publicans were

Holcombe Church and School c1903

Plant Farm, 1976

School House, Dundee Lane

charging too much rent for their pitches - 2s for a large stall was a lot of money then. But the sports were still held in Holcombe village and that year there was plenty of excitement. In the first place, they were three hours late in starting because most of the villagers had gone off to follow the Holcombe Harriers on foot. They went twenty miles to kill four hares, so even if you didn't go all the way, it was quite a walk. Nearly 600 people came to watch the wrestling match in a meadow behind the Shoulder of Mutton, and a fight broke out among the spectators in the middle of it. It took several policemen to break up another fight during the high jump competition, and there were also various races and a prize of a leg of mutton for being the quickest to climb a 35-foot pole; this last event was won by a Ramsbottom boy who did it in 37 seconds. In the evening, everybody retired to the pubs to get drunk. And according to an old man who was present, even this was tame compared to the early days of the century, when being 'the best fighter, runner, drinker, and liar' made you the best man in Holcombe.

Nowadays, the violence of the 19th century is forgotten and the village is peaceful once more. Fortunately, it is also a conservation area, so there is some hope that its seventeenth century charm will be retained.

EDENFIELD

If you follow the River Irwell far enough north of Bury, you come to Ewood Bridge, a 200-year-old, two-arched structure built by 'Blind Jack of Knaresborough'. I don't think there's much at Ewood apart from the bridge and the railway station. That, of course, used to be on the East Lancashire railway line on the way to Rawtenstall. Its full title was 'Ewood Bridge and Edenfield' and it is the latter portion of the area I am now interested in.

Edenfield consists mostly of a long, straggling street of typical Rossendale houses, together with pubs, shops, one or two works and a very ancient church. Above the village are the lofty fells of Scout Moor whose rolling tracts have a beauty all their own. High up there is Waugh's Well, a stone monument with a likeness sculpted in bronze of the famous Lancashire poet, Edwin Waugh. Sadly, vandals

Ewood Bridge and Edenfield Station

Edwin Waugh

have sliced off a bit of his nose, but otherwise he is remarkably well preserved and looks out over the valley with a keen eye. In a literary career spanning some forty years he poured forth prose, verse, songs, tales and character sketches; many were humorous, some excited pity but all illustrated the life of Lancashire's towns and villages and abundant use was made of dialect. His song, 'Come Whoam to thi Childer and Me', written in 1856, sold thousands of copies in penny broadsheets.

Waugh was a sturdy, independent and plain spoken Lancashire man, but alas, there were long periods when he drank excessively. However, he was fortunate in his friend and counsellor Joseph Chatwood, a native of Edenfield who knew the fells and foothills of Scout Moor. In order to keep him away from his drinking companions, Joseph persuaded the intemperate genius to stay for a few weeks at Fo' Edge Farm amid the rolling moorland. It was a great success, the writer's health improved and in those remote surroundings he produced some of his best work.

Chatwood had been in business as an architect and surveyor in Union Square, Bury, since 1849 and presided on at least two occasions when Waugh visited the town. There was a dinner for the radical Sam Bamford at the Albion Hotel in 1858, when Waugh responded to the toast of 'the Lancashire Poets'. I don't know whether Joseph Chatwood was there then, but five years

F L Tavare postcard showing the original Waugh's Well and Fo' Edge Farm, with Waugh inset

later he chaired a meeting at the Athenaeum when Waugh read his own work, and he presided again in March 1865 when Waugh and Ben Brierley performed there together. He was also instrumental in building the first Waugh's Well (it was renewed on its centenary in 1966).

There are, of course, many interesting beauty spots around Edenfield, among them the lightly-wooded banks of Dearden Clough, through which the Dearden Brook flows down into Stubbins. There was once a 'lido' here, an open-air baths where you could swim in cool waters on hot summer days. Built in 1901, it was open to the public seven days a week and the entry fee was 2d. The area where the water was collected was named, appropr-

Edenfield Baths

iately enough, 'Plunge', and you can still walk along Plunge Road to follow the brook up the valley.

The third annual gala in 1903 was a very grand occasion, with seats and stands erected to accommodate an audience of 350. Among the attractions was the aforementioned David Billington, who beat a Bacup man by a length and a half over 1,000 yards, despite giving him a start. Other events were a pillow fight, a polo match and an exhibition of fancy swimming by Little Jess of Bury, the eleven-year-old son of Bury Baths superintendent. Afterwards the swimmers were entertained to tea in Edenfield Co-op Hall.

I cannot say when the lido was closed; the swimming club was still going in 1914, with 115 members by the end of the year and enough confidence in the future to spend £18.2.0d on repairs and putting up a new bridge. But the chilliness of the spring water from the high moors combined with a season or two of inclement summer weather put an end to one or two other lidos I know about, and this one probably met the same fate.

Below this point, the waters of Dearden Brook were used for industrial purposes by several concerns, of which the most famous was probably Turnbull and Stockdale's at Stubbins. (It was Mr William Stockdale who presided at the swimming gala mentioned above.) The partnership was formed in Doctors Lane, Bury, in 1881 but the business expanded rapidly

Rose Bank Works, Stubbins, once the home of Turnbull and Stockdale's calico printing enterprise

and in 1896 they took over the Rose Bank works and practically rebuilt it. Eventually the calico prints produced at Rose Bank became world famous. Mr Turnbull was born at Blackford Bridge and educated at Radcliffe, where he learned to become a machine printer. He died in 1915, much regretted in the neighbourhood, and the flags flew at half mast over the works and in many other places. Mr Stockdale was a native of Bury and, like his partner, was prominent in local affairs, serving on both Ramsbottom Urban District Council and on the County Council. At the time of writing the old sign still stands at the entrance to the Rose Bank site, but sadly much of the works is now derelict and the rest used by smaller industrial concerns.

The Pack Horse, Edenfield, now renamed the Tophams Arms. Dick Nuttall stabled his horses in the white building next door

The sundial, Edenfield Church - 'Time devours all things'.

Edenfield itself is an old settlement and has been identified with the 'Aytefeld' visited by the Royal Commissioners in 1552; the only goods possessed were one vestment and a bell. I had heard that a famous bell, dated 1654, could be seen in 'God's Acre', so I went to look for it. Passing through a venerable lych-gate into the churchyard, I found a very ancient church and I could see it was called 'God's Acre', but I couldn't find a bell. I did see, however, an old sundial in the church wall, where church-goers of bygone days could see if they were late. Then an old gentleman informed me that the bell was stolen, was later returned and is now safe and secure within the church itself.

I wanted to know how old the church was and I was told to ask Mrs Whittaker, so I went along to her house. Here I found the front door open and a glass-windowed vestibule inscribed with a picture of a splendid shire horse, which sent me off on a different historical track. Mrs Whittaker turned out to be from the same family as J & J Whittaker, who were the carting agents for the Lancashire & Yorkshire Railway at Ramsbottom. My father was a carter and worked for them at the turn of the century. Earlier still he was a 'Manchester carter' for 'Dick' Nuttall of Edenfield, whose stables are still there, next to the Pack Horse hotel. (The new sign proclaims that the pub is the Tophams Arms, but the windows still say 'Pack Horse'.) My father would take four horses with a load of cloth to Manchester about one o'clock in the morning, getting his breakfast at a public house where a convoy of carters would be waiting. The landlord had a very large frying pan and everything went into it - bacon, eggs, sausage, cheese, kippers, the lot - to be shared by the hungry carters.

I did get to know, by the way, that the church tower was built in 1614 and that the present church dates mostly from 1778.

Edenfield Church as it is today

𝕊𝕊𝕊𝕊𝕊𝕊𝕊𝕊𝕊𝕊𝕊𝕊𝕊𝕊𝕊𝕊𝕊𝕊𝕊𝕊𝕊𝕊

RADCLIFFE

One of the places which became part of Metropolitan Bury in 1974 is the former borough of Radcliffe, whose mediaeval origins have been somewhat obscured by later industry. The manor of Radcliffe is mentioned in the Domesday survey of 1086 and the remains of Radcliffe Tower, now scheduled as an ancient monument, can be seen in the south-east corner of the borough. The direct male line of the Radcliffe family died out in the early 16th century and the manor passed to another branch who were Earls of Sussex. The family's interest in it ceased when the third Earl, Thomas Radcliffe, sold the manor to Richard Assheton, lord of the adjoining manor of Middleton. When the Assheton heiress married Sir Thomas Egerton, the manor went to them, but the tower was probably not continuously occupied after the Radcliffes left and apparently not lived in at all after 1765, so that it gradually fell into decay. The original tower dated from Norman times, as did parts of the parish church, though it has been restored at various times. There is also an ancient tithe barn.

Artist's impression of Radcliffe Tower as it was in the early seventeenth century

Apart from that, little is left of the mediaeval town, and indeed some of the mills which followed have gone too now. The Peels, the Bealeys and the Cromptons all had works flourishing around the area.

Not far behind them were the Mellors, of whom Colonel John James Mellor is best remembered in the neighbourhood. He was born in Oldham on 12th August 1830, the youngest of fifteen children. At the age of 17 he began work in a spinning mill to learn the business and later went into partnership with his brother Jonathan (died 1890) at Bamford, then at Heywood. In 1865 the lease of the Bamford mill ran out and the two brothers built the large mills at Warth. They were among the few firms to stay open during the cotton famine and the Mellors prided themselves on keeping close, friendly relations with their workpeople. In 1901 Colonel Mellor celebrated fifty years in business by giving a fete at Belle Vue for all his workers and expressed his feelings towards them: 'My late brother and partner before his death charged me to tell his workpeople that he had always regarded them not as hired servants, but as friends. That is a sentiment I shall carry with me to the grave. During my fifty years as an employer of labour there has never been a strike among my workpeople.' That the feeling was mutual is indicated by the wording of the testimonial with which he was presented on his 81st birthday: 'To Col John James Mellor, JP, DL.
Dear sir, – We, the workpeople of Messrs J and JJ Mellor Ltd, the Warth Mills, Bury, desire

The parish church, Radcliffe

to tender to you our heartiest congratulations on the attainment of your 81st birthday and also of 60 years of business life. We wish to express our great regard and the affection in which you are held by us all. We take this opportunity of recording our appreciation of your consideration and interest in our welfare, and sincerely hope that both you and Mrs Mellor may be long spared to enjoy a well-earned rest.

Signed on behalf of the work-people,
JOHN ECCLES
JOHN ROBINSON
THOS. HOWARTH
THOS. BAINBRIDGE
Warth Mills Bury
Aug 12th, 1911.'

Beyond his business commitments Colonel Mellor was much involved in the affairs of Radcliffe throughout his career. He commanded a battalion of Volunteers, built a school at Warth Fold to give non-denominational education to the children of the neighbourhood and gave generously of his time and money to many local churches, though he himself worshipped at Stand. He was a JP for nearly fifty years and Member of Parliament for Radcliffe-cum-Farnworth from 1895 to 1900. He died in 1916 at the age of 86 and was commemorated by Mellor Hall and Mellor Street.

Advertisement from the Prestwich and Whitefield Guide, 25/11/1921

About the time that the canal was being built, Mellor Street was known as Market Street and the Radcliffe theatre stood nearby. It was a wooden building which was blown down in a severe storm and just before the turn of the century more modern premises were built on Mellor Street. These were owned by George Testo Sante, who was a real character and

a great showman, and he called his theatre the Grand Opera House.

An American by birth, he had joined a travelling circus at the age of ten and in middle life had come to England and settled in Chorley. He opened a theatre there before coming to Radcliffe and later built a picture palace at Besses and one on Kenyon Street, Radcliffe, as well as the theatre. All three were put up for sale in 1916 but the reserve prices were not reached and they were withdrawn. I don't know what happened to them after that; Mr Sante died later the same year and presumably his wife took over his business affairs.

She was also a trouper and show artist and trod the boards regularly. It is said that she was the boss of any production and that the cast, and her husband as well, were terrified of her. Still, they did hold a party for her and gave her a silver cruet and salt cellars when she retired in September 1916, a few weeks before her husband's demise.

By 1917 the opera house title had been dropped and the place was known as the Grand Theatre, then the Palace, but failed to attract sufficient audiences. It was sold in 1923 for £7,000 'and nothing for goodwill' after being shut for some time. Its fortunes changed after a grand reopening on November 19th of that year as the Coliseum Cinema. Prices ranged from 7d in the gallery to 1s10d in the dress circle for 'early doors', or 5d to 1s6d for 'ordinary doors', and the first show was a musical comedy

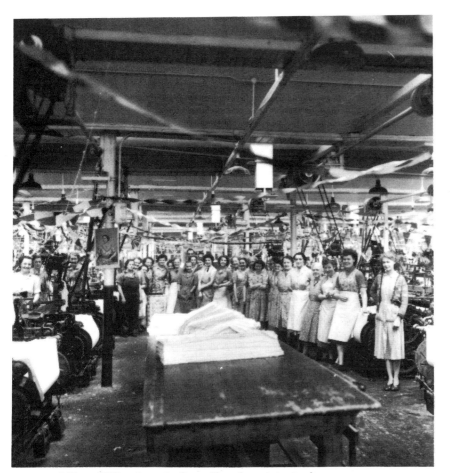

Warth Mills, 1953, just before Macphersons took over

called 'His Lucky Wife'. A local writer described the redecorated theatre as 'a dream of beauty'.

I don't know whether it was or not, but I do remember going there about 1927, when it was a cinema and music hall. Sammy Dickenson, the strongest lad in Bury, worked at Hacking's with a few of my mates, so we all joined the Health and Strength League. One of the world's strongest men - I think his name was Herman Gorman - was appearing at the Coliseum and we went to see him. We had to watch a film first and then he came on to the stage. He was a tremendous chap and his greatest feat was to hold on his shoulders a roundabout on which twelve full-sized men sat for a ride. The Coliseum later became a regular cinema until 1945, when it was gutted by fire.

In the 1920s the cotton trade was very unstable and Mellor's old mill closed for a while, but very soon opened up again as Warth Mill. I had just left school and applied for a job there as office boy, but wasn't successful. When the Second World War started I was living very close to the mill and I remember one beautiful Sunday

Blackburn Street, Radcliffe. The three nearest buildings on the left hand side are, from left to right, the National Westminster Bank, the Maypole Dairy and W Newton's tripe shop

morning in May when the Army moved in and started to knock parts of it down and rebuild other portions: the Government had requisitioned it and converted it into a camp for internees. Quite a few of the inmates were classical musicians and singers and on summer Sunday evenings many an impromptu performance could be heard from within the old mill. Later, prisoners-of-war arrived

regularly, and we saw German and Italian soldiers and airmen exercising themselves in the barbed wire compound.

When the military left, the old mill opened up again briefly, then the huge paint manufacturing firm of Donald Macpherson & Co took over the old mill, adding yet another industry to those which have dominated the area.

AINSWORTH, WALSHAW & DISTRICT

AINSWORTH

Radcliffe once had no fewer than seven railway stations. Of these, Ainsworth Road Halt was probably the least important, but the village of Ainsworth to which the road led has a most interesting history.

Still known as Cockey Moor to older people, Ainsworth is on the old road from Bolton to Bury and a short length of Well Street, part of the original road before the turnpike was built, remains. If you happen to pass that way in romantic mood, it is easy to imagine the note of the distant post-horn as the mail coach neared the village, and the whinnying of the horses as they were brought to a halt in the courtyard of the inn.

The Duke William Inn still stands where it was built some 250 years ago when George II, the last monarch to lead his troops into battle, was on the throne. His second living son, William, then sixteen years of age and his parents' favourite, had been made Duke of Cumberland some ten years earlier. Apparently he was esteemed by the owners of the new hostelry, who named it after him. It was a splendid choice, for in later years he became an eminent soldier, though he was also said to be proud and unforgiving and fond of war for its own sake. Feted as a hero after his defeat of the Scottish

The Duke William, Ainsworth, 1976

rebels at Culloden, he became less popular when tales of his soldiers' treatment of the Scots after the battle reached English ears and earned him the nickname, 'Butcher Cumberland'.

Cheek by jowl with the Duke William is the Unitarian Chapel, built in 1715 and later enlarged (1773) and altered (1845). Close by is another old building, now a house, with four stone steps, convenient for worshippers who arrived at the chapel on horseback. Here too is the anciently-named Oaks Nook and Hook's Cottage, bearing the date 1773 on its lintel. The road continues alongside quaint cottages with old-world gardens and here is Anchor Lane, which some say was the centre of the village. Near the junction with Well Street stood the Anchor Inn, where stage coaches halted, 'it being a principal house of call' in 1742; this would seem to indicate an even earlier inn than the Duke William.

Unitarian Chapel, Ainsworth

Well Street is about a hundred yards away from the present busy main road, and the motorists whizzing past miss the agreeable features of the village. On the opposite side of the road is the parish church and passing through the lych-gate and by the posts of the ancient stocks, visitors find the tiniest of churches. There was already a chapel here in 1515 and although it was largely rebuilt in 1831/32, parts of the building are probably more than 500 years old. Still tiny and mellowed, though not quite

Ainsworth, or 'Cockey Moor', Church

Hook's Cottage, Ainsworth, 1982

as old as the church, is the village school, where 'Owd Sumner' was one of Cockey Moor's most respected characters. He was the village schoolmaster for some 40 years, retired in 1916 and died in 1946 at the grand old age of 94. When he started at the low-roofed school in 1876, it had one stone-floored room and all the pupils were in one class without regard to age or ability. Slates were used for writing on and half-timers often fell asleep during lessons after a hard morning's work.

For some years education in Ainsworth was quite a family affair. In 1879 a Miss Catchpool came to the school as the first lady teacher, married Mr Sumner two years later and was head of the infants' school until 1914. Their son-in-law, Mr W Thompson, took over as headmaster when the old man retired and was there until the

1930s and a Miss Ethel Sumner, presumably a daughter, retired from the staff in the 1940s.

After his retirement, Mr Sumner was not idle. In 1918 he became a member of the Rural District Council and Bury Board of Guardians, when Ainsworth and Radcliffe were joined together he served on Radcliffe District Council, and when Radcliffe became a borough in its own right he was made an alderman. Alderman William Sumner probably had many maxims in his long and informative career, but I believe his favourite was 'Remember the "magic 12".' When it goes dark, subtract that hour from 12 to find what time it will be light again.

Ainsworth School, 1976

The hamlet of Starling, between Ainsworth and Bury, was probably busier at the time of the Napoleonic Wars than it is now. In Street Lane there were three cottages where handloom weaving was carried on, and it has been said that much of the cloth was used to make uniforms for soldiers who fought at Waterloo. There were several coal pits nearby, a quarry and on the way to Walshaw was Lowercroft Bleach Works. The works was owned by successive generations of the Whitehead family, who lived at Haslam Hey close by and were much respected in the district. Their benevolent legacy can be seen in the beauty of some of Bury's monuments and gardens, and in the development of some of the villages around. Best known of Henry Whitehead's gifts are the Elton Recreation Ground, opened

Haslam Hey

in 1886, and the Whitehead Memorial Tower, given in memory of his elder brother Walter in 1914. But he was also responsible for rebuilding Ainsworth Village School and made many smaller donations: church pulpits; pictures and artefacts to the Art Gallery and so on. This kind of generosity became a family tradition.

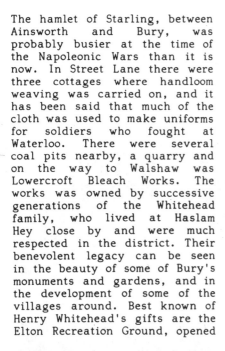

Councillor William Sumner

Henry Whitehead

WALSHAW

Today four roads join the hub of Walshaw and traffic streams through incessantly, but if you walk slowly around there is much to evoke the past two hundred years. Walshaw Mill, still in use but now a mixture of the old and new, is overlooked by Pennington Street and its rows of 19th century cottages. Around the 1840s two families, the Holts and the Haworths, practically monopolised the cotton trade in Walshaw.

Jesse Haworth is particularly well remembered. He was a manufacturer of fustians and swansdown and Christ Church, Walshaw was erected in his memory by his sister Nancy and his nephew, the Rev John Gorell Haworth, who worked in Jesse's mill before being ordained.

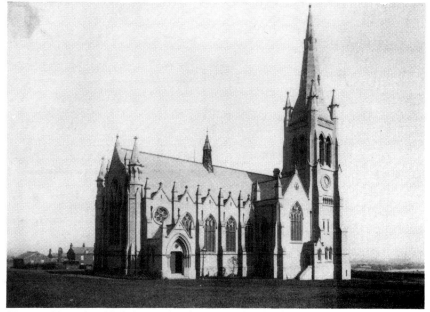

Christ Church, Walshaw, built in memory of Jesse Haworth

James Haworth & Sons was for many years the main source of employment in the village and Jesse and his brothers and sister are said to have been brought up almost opposite, in the house which is now the Victoria Inn. Here, in the early nineteenth century, their father James carried on business as a shopkeeper and manufacturer of cotton cloth, giving out work to handloom weavers; no doubt the children learnt something of the trade by helping out. Jesse Haworth was 83 when he died in 1887, leaving his wealth to his nephew. He seems to have been a man of generous intentions but one who did not like to see his money wasted, judging by what the Rev John Gorell Haworth said of him when the church was opened: he 'would nearly, if not altogether' have built the church thirty years earlier, 'but for the indolence and indifference of the clergyman in the district at that time.'

It was a good thing for the cotton trade in Walshaw that the Victoria Inn existed. Many years later, when the mill was no longer owned by the Haworths, the 'Vic's' landlady, Mrs Platt, spotted a fire breaking out on the third storey about ten o'clock one Monday evening. Of course, this was 1911 and it took longer to call out the emergency services in those days. She told her cousin, George Mellalieu, who told Mr Thomas Holt, who got a telephone message sent to the Fire Brigade from Mr Smethurst's house at High Bank. By the time all these people had been notified, flames were bursting through the upper windows and the glow in the sky could be seen for miles. According to the paper, thousands flocked to the village to watch, nearly blocking the roads. Despite this, the Fire Brigade's three engines managed to stop the fire spreading to Holts' mill next door and had it under control by 3.00am. The workforce helped, taking the horses to safety and then using the stables to store cloth and yarn moved from the warehouses. In the event, each end of the mill was saved but a large four-storey building was completely destroyed and the weaving sheds damaged. 460 were thrown out of work, but it was hoped to re-employ the weavers before long. Meanwhile, it cost the Bury, Radcliffe and District Weavers' Association over £100 a week in relief payments to those who were insured. But without Mrs Platt's sharp eyesight, things could have been a lot worse.

After two years the loyal workforce got some recognition for their prompt action in helping to save the stock, but the way it was announced would not go down well with trade unionists today! On 5th July 1913 it was said that because of insurance and the workers' actions in helping to minimise the loss, 'the shareholders did not feel it. The workpeople were the only ones to suffer, hence, after a fairly good run, the directors have decided it will be a reasonable and gracious act to present them all with a week's extra pay on the eve of next holiday.'

The other main Walshaw firm,

Pennington Street, with part of Walshaw Mill on the right

William Holt & Sons, shut down in 1942 after nearly 150 years trading. Their PK bedspreads were internationally famous and were used in the world's largest hotel, the Pennsylvania in America. In fact, the company was ordered to close by the Cotton Controller and the directors, Mr Thomas Holt of Haslam Hey and Mr J W Holt of High Bank, were understandably annoyed. They complained, 'through the closure the Services do not gain the help of one man, for all our employés are old in the service of the firm,' but to no avail and production ceased in the first week of April.

Walshaw is an ancient settlement and some buildings were there even before the era of the Holts and the Haworths, in the days when the roads were narrow and unpaved and the place so serene that inhabitants could actually hear the brook babbling by. The 'Olde Village Shoppe' on Bank Street, which now sells newspapers, stationery and other things, was there then, though the Co-op next door was not built until 1891. It is a Co-op no longer but the stone inscriptions above the shops are still visible: 'Grocer', 'Clogger' and in the centre 'News Room'; the word 'Butcher' is covered by a modern sign. This was not the first Co-op in Walshaw, by the way - there had been one in 1866, when the society was in its very early days.

Fairs were once held on a site not far from the White Horse Hotel and villagers would enjoy the swing boats, ginger snap stalls and side shows. Not far away either was 'th'ustage stile', used by the old cattle dealers to clinch their bargains; when the deal was made, hands were placed on the post and the words 'I pledge thee my oath' were said.

Colonel G E Wike, Mayor 1897-99

Elton House

ELTON

ELTON HOUSE

In the early eighteenth century Elton, now a township within Bury, was a separate community straggling alongside the western edge of the River Irwell. Most of its roads were simple tracks, undulating and rutted, but the main highway was wide enough for the mail coach to negotiate twice a day as it passed the farms and fields of Cockey Moor, Starling and Elton Fold.

One of the dwellings in the once rural hamlet of Elton Fold has withstood the rigours and modifications of 250 years. A substantial stone building just off Ainsworth Road, Elton House, now a nursing home, has a datestone above the door, 'PWA 1731', which indicates that the house's history goes back further than its facade implies. The front windows suggest Victorian origin but those at the back, and the kitchens inside, are apparently early Georgian.

I assume that the letters 'PWA' refer to William Plant and his wife Anne. The influential Plant family had farms at Ainsworth and Woodhill, and who can say that a branch was not flourishing at Elton House? It is well known that the family owned lands in Holcombe village in 1734 and a farmhouse was built in 1739 with a similar 'PWA' datestone.

The first written record of Elton House appears to be the 1841 census, which reveals that the house was occupied by Samuel Rothwell, a bleacher, and his family. The business progressed favourably but three years later, when the Whiteheads of Lowercroft wanted to buy Samuel out, he took up their offer and went to live in Brandlesholme Hall.

John Whitehead moved into Elton House, an ideal spot for his interest in cattle, for there were plenty of fields around. Apparently he built the adjoining farm and added to the house a number of cottages, perhaps for his farmhands or his servants, for he had a large family to occupy his mansion; the aforementioned Henry Whitehead, Bury's benefactor, was one of his sons.

John was born in 1815 in the old house at Haslam Hey, built in 1647 and occupied by his family from time immemorial. His father, also named John, was still living there when John junior was at Elton House and his diaries show that he too was as much interested in cattle as in bleaching - except for one item, repeated on each anniversary from Friday, December 5th 1856: 'Paid for reservoir burst of 1852 - £5,650 - damage and law'. The Whiteheads' lodges, well known to generations of Eltonians and others beyond the township, were being built in 1852. The lower lodge had been completed and the middle one was well on the way when, on Saturday December 5th, it burst and the torrent of water swept over the entire area. It was a calamity and the damage was estimated at £35,000, so I reckon John senior came out of it very well.

At any rate, the family fortunes were sufficiently secure for Henry Whitehead to have the old house at Haslam Hey demolished after his grandfather died in 1876, and to have a new mansion built on the site.

When John Whitehead junior left, Elton House had a succession of influential occupants. In 1880 Colonel George Edward Wike lived there, a truly remarkable man. In 1874 he went into business with his brother William as woollen merchants and manufacturers, first at Openshaw Fold and then at Chesham. Quite an athlete in his youth, he was at one time secretary of the Holcombe Hunt and played for Bury Cricket Club. He was also musical, President of the Athenaeum Operatic Society and during the twenty years he lived at Elton House, organist at All Saints Church. An active churchman, he was warden of St Paul's for a while when he moved over to Danesmoor, and he represented the diocese at the National Assembly of the Church of England. He was prominent in municipal affairs, a councillor from 1890 and Mayor for two years from 1897; during this time he founded the Mayor's Charity.

With all these and many other responsibilities, he found time to be Commanding Officer of the Bury Volunteer Battalion from 1900 to 1907 and was instrumental in bringing in funds for the magnificent extension to the Drill Hall, opened by the Duke of Connaught in 1907. About tea time on 13th October 1906 Colonel Wike himself laid the foundation stone of this splendid work, having set himself to raise £7,500 before doing so. At five to one that day he had £7,488 and got a promise of a further £50 at one o'clock! He was made a Freeman of the Borough in 1911.

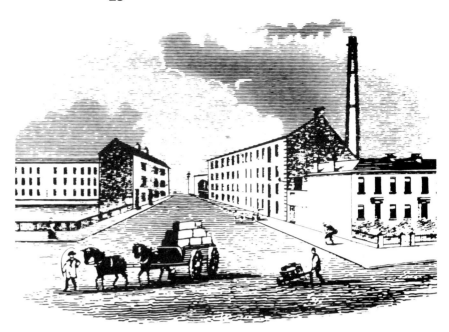

The Wikes' mill, Drake Street

During and after the First World War he put his fund raising talents to use on behalf of the Prisoner of War Fund and later the Lancashire Fusiliers Compassionate and War Memorial Fund. He died suddenly, aged 74, on 2nd December 1921. The lines he wrote about his work for the Fund a few hours before his death are characteristic of him and an inspiring epitaph: 'I cannot help making, it may be a final effort, on behalf of the ex-soldiers. The winter will bring many privations and hardships, but when it is over we shall, I believe, be in smoother waters. We are in the aftermath of a great war and all are passing through trying times, but we must face them as best we can, and having done so we shall never regret any sacrifice we may make.'

By the time Colonel Wike became Mayor, Samuel Taylor had taken over Elton House. Mr Taylor started a small shop in Silver Street, at first selling fancy goods and later sporting goods and boy scout uniforms; I got mine in 1922. The firm, still run by his grandson, celebrated its centenary in 1979 and today Sam Taylor's has developed into a large establishment in the Haymarket.

An interesting story connected with Elton House in the present century was told to me by Mrs Hulme of Radcliffe. The house was then occupied by a very gracious lady named Mrs Kay and her daughter Constance. They had three servants and the parlour maid was courting a railwayman who worked at Bolton Street Station. The couple came from Shropshire originally and they decided to get married in their home town, but when the time came they couldn't get there. There was a big rail strike on and they had to postpone the happy day. However, they did marry eventually and in due course the young parlour maid became the mother of Mrs Hulme.

More than seventy years ago I lived with my parents at Lower Hinds, a hamlet on the outskirts of Bury, and in the eighteenth century Robert Peel built one of his mills there. I knew it well in the days when it was owned by the Bury Wool Company, processing the wool taken off sheep skins. In 1935 Benjamin Ovenden started a much larger fellmongering concern there and moved into Elton House, yet another character in its chequered career. The works went from

Opening of the Drill Hall extension, 1907

strength to strength and although he is no longer there, it now covers the entire area; in one portion of the site are still the bricks and doorsteps of a row of old cottages.

I visited Elton House some time ago and was shown round by Mrs Kirkman, who then lived there. The house was in remarkably good condition for its 250-plus years, with bright spacious rooms at the front. Another room had been added by using one of the cottages, but the kitchen quarters revealed its real age, Unfortunately, no-one seems to know who built it. Even the datestone doesn't help, for it is thought that this was put in after a remodelling and that the original bits of the house are older still.

Haymarket Street, 1971

ELTON RESERVOIR

When the Manchester, Bolton and Bury Canal was being planned, some local industrialists became apprehensive. They needed water from the River Irwell for their mills and this new waterway was to follow the course of the river closely as it approached Bury. Would it siphon off their valuable supplies? The difficulty was overcome when the canal company promised, among other things, to ensure a regular supply of their own by constructing a reservoir at Elton and building a feeder to fill it with water collected from much higher up the river.

Over the years, in addition to fulfilling its main purpose, the reservoir has been a source of pleasure to countless Bury and Radcliffe residents. Shooting, fishing, rowing and sailing were among the activities encouraged there. In earlier times its seclusion and serenity prompted a group of gentlemen to form a club which would be an ideal retreat for them. Apart from the usual indoor club facilities, there was an opportunity for sporting types to shoot at waterfowl: geese and wild ducks, grebes, herons and divers could all be seen there in those days. Rowing boats appeared, propelled by energetic young gentlemen, some of whom would have persuaded a lady associate to accompany them. She, of course, would just sit leisurely

in the boat, dabbling her fingers in the water.

There were fish in the reservoir and in 1858 Henry Vickerman, one of the club members, formed the Bury Angling Association. About sixty fishermen joined and Lord Wilton, who owned much land around Bury at that time, allowed them to use the reservoir in return for an annual fee of 5s. R N Philips, the local MP, gave a donation of £5, so the anglers got a very good start and were able to appoint a competent bailiff.

On the side nearest the canal the reservoir is banked and topped by a stout stone wall. Alongside is a rough roadway, a short cut between Bury and Radcliffe which forms a 'promenade' where people from both towns can linger on summer days, or walk briskly as a fresh breeze whips the water into wavelets. On good days at the turn of the century, and particularly on Sunday afternoons, the reservoir would take on the appearance of a seaside rendezvous, with happy boaters, club members and their ladies taking tea on the lawn.

In 1902, however, those happy days along the reservoir embankment were threatened by the Lancashire & Yorkshire Railway, who were by then the owners. They decided to close the embankment to the public and erected barriers at both ends. But the people of Bury and Radcliffe had no intention of letting the railway get away with this. The barriers were torn down and re-erected time and time again, and eventually

Elton Reservoir and boathouse

the railway company resorted to the law.

So the citizens of Radcliffe did the same. A spirited champion named John Davenport formed an eight-man committee and a town's meeting was called. There was no doubt that they had public support and the 'Reservoir Right of Way Defence Fund' was begun. The final onslaught on the barriers was witnessed by about 600 of the populace, with police and solicitors standing by. The case that followed was held at the Manchester Spring Assizes and the railway company lost. They lost again when they went to London to appeal to the Royal Court of Justice and finally the House of Lords upheld the decision. That was in 1906, and the right of way has remained ever since.

Today, the embankment is often thronged with people watching the sailing and yacht racing which is much in evidence. The modern club is one of the most successful of its kind in the country and some of the sailors have achieved national fame.

Bury New Road, Whitefield, with Woodward's confectioner's on the left

POINTS SOUTH

WHITEFIELD

Whitefield and Prestwich, two of the towns which are now part of Bury Metro, stand on the A56 road to Manchester, used by thousands of Bury people day after day. I too worked in Manchester for most of my life and in the course of passing through these little towns, at one time ancient villages, picked up quite a few tales of their history. However, I have written about most of these before, so perhaps a few personal reminiscences may be of interest.

I got to know Whitefield particularly well at night. My job as a railway goods clerk in Manchester entailed lengthy spells of regular shift work and the first one of these was at London Road just before the war, when I worked from 6.30pm to 3.00am during the week and from 1.00am to 7.00am on Saturdays. Salford Corporation ran an hourly bus service throughout the night and this was my means of getting home, but in those days it only went as far as Whitefield and I had to walk the rest. I was living in Bolton Road then, but quickly moved house into Redvales and could get home from Whitefield in 25 minutes. I soon discovered a fellow night traveller who worked on a newspaper and also lived in Bury, and inevitably we strode home together. We discovered a mutual interest in football and the journey was never long enough to finish our discussions. When we were lucky, a third football fanatic by the name of Horrocks would be passing in his car and give us a lift; I still see him sometimes, shopping in Bury's precinct.

Shortly after this, I spent five years in the army and when I was demobbed went back to London Road, only to find that railway wages were not keeping pace with those in other industries. I needed more money to meet domestic expenses and there was nothing for it but to go back on nights. I did that trip from Whitefield to home for another six years, but I was

Whitefield Station c1929

ten years older now and the journey time had increased to 35 minutes. I tried often, but I couldn't do it in less.

Thus, I knew Whitefield very well – in the dark! One day, when I was working in the Staff Office at London Road, the Chief, knowing I had to come through Whitefield on my way to work, asked me to call at the house of a missing motor driver and try to find him. I located the first address, but the lady who answered the door said, 'He doesn't live here now, he's gone to Hillock,' and I hadn't a clue where to go next. I'd never heard of Hillock! However, she directed me up an unpaved lane nearby and when I reached the place I was astonished. It was one of the most ancient little villages I had ever seen. On each side of the lane stood a row of cottages, their little gardens all neat and tidy, with climbing ivy and 'roses round the door'. An idyllic spot, with its own little chapel and the Albert Inn, a typical country tavern. I never found the motor driver and forgot all about him, but I'll never forget Hillock. It has gone now under a huge housing estate, and a modern public house has replaced the Albert.

The original Whitefield was only a small portion of the Manor of Pilkington, which also included Outwood, Ringley, Unsworth and of course many little hamlets like Stand and Besses o'th'Barn. The latter is probably most famous for its brass band, thinking of which brings back nostalgic memories from 70 or more years ago. Brass bands were in their heyday and Besses were the greatest. Had they not just toured the world? I went to see

The old Albert Inn, Hillock

and hear them play on a beautiful summer Sunday evening at Gigg Lane football ground. The soloist was Rushworth, the famous cornetist, and he stilled the ground to silence. I cannot remember the piece, but the encore was his usual one, 'I Passed by your Window' and during it, you could have heard a pin drop.

The ancient Pilkington family, Lords of the Manor, were around in Norman times and for 400 years were settled at Stand. However, they chose to support Richard III at the battle of Bosworth Field in 1485 and when Richard was killed and the new king, Henry VII, took the throne, he confiscated the extensive Pilkington lands and handed them over to his stepfather, Sir Thomas Stanley,

whom he later created first Earl of Derby.

By this time the Pilkingtons' hall was nearly two hundred years old and the Stanleys weren't satisfied with it. In the early 16th century they built a new, two-storey house next door, named this Stand Hall and sold the old hall off. It was licensed as a chapel for a time in the 17th century but by 1852 was being used as a cowshed. Meanwhile, the Stanleys' 'new house' had been demolished and its replacement had burnt down only five years later, in 1840. It was the home of the Earl of Derby's agent, Mr Statter, at the time. When yet another replacement was built in the 1860s, it was occupied by a gentleman who was soon to be decidedly unpopular with Mr Statter, Richard Rome Bealey. This house in black and white Tudor style still stands, called Stand Old Hall. The really old hall was still being used as a farm building until the 1960s, when it was taken down.

The difference between Mr Bealey and Mr Statter arose partly because Mr Statter was too good at his job. So keen was he to protect his master's interests that he made himself very unpopular with His Lordship's tenants, and in the 1860s the spirited citizens of Whitefield had the temerity to take him to court over a right of way dispute.

It all began when Mr Statter closed the path from Park Lane to Holebottom and tried to prevent Mr Winterbottom, who lived at Woodlands, near Park Lane, from going that way. The

Besses o'th'Barn Band, with flags indicating the extent of their travels

agent couldn't prove his right to close the path to Mr Winterbottom's satisfaction and at a public meeting, held at Park Lane School and chaired by Mr Bealey, the citizens aired their grievances. Mr Statter had persecuted a farmer on Ringley Road, had made the Young Men's Institute take down a gym which they had erected at some expense, had destroyed a well at Unsworth. This was the last straw and the people of Whitefield fought back. As fast as he put barriers up, they chopped them down, almost weekly, and when some of them were charged with riot the magistrates threw the case out of court. In the end, as the only way of settling the matter, Mr Winterbottom decided to sue Mr Statter for damages – the three or four pounds he'd paid for the axe and the wages of the men who demolished the barriers!

The case was heard on 21st March 1867 at Manchester Assizes and an impressive parade of Whitefield senior citizens appeared as witnesses for both sides. James Booth – 'ninety if I live until next July' – said that for as long as he could remember people who lived in Park Lane went to Prestwich that way; it had also been used by weavers at Stand taking their goods to Manchester market. John Booth (82, no relation) recalled Park Lane weavers going to Mr Clegg's factory near Prestwich Church that way. His brother David (87) had worked for a butcher at Besses o'th'Barn as a boy and had delivered meat that way. He also admitted to using it for 'lovers' walks' when he was a bit older! And so on, and so on – there must

The present Stand Old Hall

have been very few elderly people in Whitefield that day!

Everyone was most careful not to blame the Earl of Derby and very polite to Mr Statter, but the evidence on his side wasn't very convincing and he lost his case. Whether Mr Winterbottom got his full damages I don't know, as that was left for a separate hearing in the Court of Exchequer. The right of way remains to this day, across Whitefield Golf Course.

I don't know whose side Mr Alfred Grundy of Underley was on in all this, but he was certainly an influential and benevolent citizen. Originally called Green Hill, his house had been built in 1805 by a nankeen manufacturer called Edward Barlow on land leased

from the Earl of Derby. In 1857 Mr Grundy bought it, renewed the lease, remodelled the house and named it Underley after his first wife's birthplace in Cumberland. He was still living there in 1890, when he gave Whitefield its park. Later the house was occupied by Samuel Walker, a Radcliffe ironfounder and in 1933 the Corporation bought it for £2,450 to use as a Town Hall; they moved in in August of that year.

〰〰〰〰〰〰〰〰〰〰〰〰〰〰〰〰〰

UNSWORTH

If you go to Unsworth via Hollins, Sunny Bank, Whitefield or even St Margaret's, you will pass through modern housing estates and the shops, public houses and few supermarkets which serve them. Whichever way you go, however, you will arrive at Unsworth Pole with its triangular Garden of Rest and war memorial cross. The lofty, pitch-pine pole was presented many generations ago by a Lord Derby and has been a village landmark for so long that nobody can remember what it was for. Nevertheless, a feast of anecdotes about Unsworth in general is available to the enquirer.

Every July Wakes the pole was greased and a copper kettle or a ham was awarded to any youth who succeeded in climbing to the top. Meanwhile, topers leaning against the black and white frontage of the 400-year-old Bay Horse Inn could laugh and scoff at their struggles. An old lady in the 1950s recalled a man named Adam Holt climbing it to put up the flag ropes for

The Bay Horse, Unsworth, 1965

celebrating the Relief of Lady-smith; I wonder if he was the last man to reach the top.

The inn, nicknamed the 'Pow', was knocked down around 1960 but I remember soaking up its mediaeval atmosphere many times. The ceiling, only a few inches above your head, had no room for any more names to be written on it. I never got the chance to see the ancient cellar, but it was said that smuggling went on there. The story goes that an old Unsworth chap bet his cronies that he could show the most money of all. He won – with a 'strike of guineas' gained from smuggling – and had to flee from their wrath.

Not far away for many years was Warburton's wheelwright's shop, later a motor body builder's. Mr Edmund Warburton founded the firm on Pole Lane in the mid-19th century, and at their peak they were producing as many as 50 wheels a day.

The most famous legend of Unsworth, of course, is that of the dragon, even today commemorated by the modern Dragon Hotel. The well-known tale of the monster which preyed on the women and children of the village, its scales impervious to bullets, records how it was slain by the resourceful Thomas Unsworth, who loaded his gun with his dagger.

One version has it that an oak tree growing on Goshen Farm was chopped down soon after-wards and that Thomas

Unsworth's dagger was used to fashion the wood into an ornate table with carved panels, one of which depicted Thomas's courageous victory. The 'Dragon Table' was made in 1618 and stood in Goshen House for more than 200 years. The last Unsworth was born there in 1882 and I believe the little girl became Elizabeth Webber, a writer of repute. Her 'Wayside and Fireside Poems' includes one called 'The old farm near the town' which tells the full story of the dragon.

In 1908 the table was sold to Mr Walter Behrens for £300 and after his death was auctioned at Christie's on 2nd December 1913 and fetched 1,000 guineas – not a bad profit in five years! In 1915 it was trans-ported to America and is said to have gone down with the ship when it was sunk by enemy action. Legend has it that it was on the Lusitania, but as she went down coming **back** from New York, it either wasn't the Lusitania or the ship wasn't sunk. I'm inclined to think that it **was** sunk, and the Unsworth table with it, and that the famous name Lusitania was added as the story was passed round by word of mouth.

Without mentioning the dragon, one writer of the past remarked that the villagers of Unsworth were somewhat primitive and simple. In support of his claim, he said that when a few of them sighted a stag which had escaped from Heaton Park, they thought it was a cow with a chair on its head!

They are not all so simple, however. An octogenarian lady I know lived in Parr Lane in her younger days and was able to describe very clearly the toffee shop which also sold the bread and pies she baked on the premises. On the fields behind was Heyworth's Higher House Farm and to climb the higher ground off Parr Lane there were the 'Cathy Steps'. I have never been able to discover the origin of this name but I believe they were the remains of the Five, or Cinq, Steps which led up to Dunkirk House. Here, in the time of the Napoleonic Wars, a group of refugees from Dunkirk settled as handloom weavers.

Indeed, handloom weaving was the main occupation in Unsworth in the eighteenth century and was phased out only as the mills were built. The story of George Fletcher shows just how sharp the Unsworth folk – and others from further afield – could be. George's mother kept a badger's shop at Lane End selling draperies, groceries and so on. He married a local girl and eventually she took over the shop and George used it to 'put out' work to weavers who would call at the shop to collect their warp and weft to weave at home. It would take them nine or ten days to complete a piece and they would get about 9 or 10s for it when it was done. In the 1830s times were hard, and the Fletchers found themselves inundated with 'presents' of a few eggs, or a chicken, from canny weavers who wanted to get their supplies quickly and hurry home to make a start before their rivals.

About 1840 George Fletcher built Kiln Croft Mill and introduced the first power looms in the district, but he is said to have been a benevolent employer who kept the shop open for some time until the mill was fully operational, so that people were not thrown out of work too suddenly. Other mills followed – Victoria Mills in 1843, Albert Mills (1850), Moss Lane (1851) and by the end of the century the really big ones like Buckley & Brennands on Castle Road. But when the Second World War broke out there were no fabrics in any of them and Buckley & Brennands was used as a barracks and to store the passenger furniture from the Queen Mary for the duration.

The Same Yet at Simister

🐚🐚🐚🐚🐚🐚🐚🐚🐚🐚🐚🐚🐚🐚🐚🐚🐚🐚

SIMISTER AND HEATON PARK

If you branch off the A56 on to Bury Old Road at Prestwich, you will come to St Margaret's Church, near Heaton Park. If you turn back towards Heywood at this point, the road takes you up Simister Lane and in the old days you would have had to pay a toll at one or two of the farmsteads to get through. The village itself looked as old as the farms, a long straggling street of century-old cottages, charming black- and white-painted shops and two ancient public houses. One of these, the Same Yet, has an unusual story to tell.

A datestone in the front of the pub tells us that it was built in 1728 by James and Mary Tetlow. Inside it looks old and is a comfortable place to partake of ale and muse on days of yore, but the style is more typical of a residential dwelling than of an eighteenth century tavern. On old maps, Simister is not named as such. The area was called Little Heaton and Tetlow Farm is clearly marked in about the right place for the pub.

The area appears to have been named after a Mr James Simister (or Somister), who settled in Little Heaton in the early part of the eighteenth century. In 1733, when his daughter Anne was born, he was registered as a yeoman and had purchased a small farm. As his affluence increased, he added three more farms and a house more suitable to his influential standing. When he died in 1780 he was a prosperous landowner and his house, the village and the lane approaching had taken his name for posterity.

Heaton Hall

I was still curious and approached the Same Yet's brewers, J W Lees & Company of Middleton, for assistance. The earlier records in their possession refer to Samuel Thorpe of Little Heaton being the owner of the dwelling known as Simister House. He appears to have died some time after 1832 and the beneficiary of his will was his son-in-law, a farmer named James Heywood. There was reference in the will to a dwelling house, one barn and about eight acres of land. The Heywood family stayed there for many years, though I believe James was callously murdered and robbed at Bury Fair in 1843.

The 1832 dwelling house was at some time converted into a beerhouse called the Seven Stars, no doubt as the village prospered. In the 1850s Simister was a silk weaving community and from most cottages could be heard the sound of treadles working the looms. On Saturday mornings the woven silk was carried in white linen bags to Manchester, where very good prices were received. It is said that this beerhouse was the one bought by J W Lees later in the century as the Same Yet. The legend of how the name changed is well known.

A travelling signwriter was given the job of repainting the sign which had been almost obliterated through bad weather. 'What shall I put on it?' he asked. 'Oh, the same yet,' replied the landlord. The signwriter took him literally and the Same Yet Inn it has been ever since.

In the days when James Simister arrived at Little Heaton the adjoining area, Heaton, was simply an extensive area of parkland, owned by the Egerton family. James would have seen the demise of both the fifth (died 1744) and sixth (died 1756) baronets, and might have caught a glimpse of their relatively modest brick-built house through the trees. The seventh baronet, Sir Thomas, was only 23 when, in 1772, he commissioned John Wyatt to rebuild and extend the old house. Today Heaton Hall is renowned not only for its classical architecture but for its collection of paintings, furniture and porcelain.

Simister Lane

Sir Thomas had married Eleanor Assheton in 1769 and they had a son and two daughters who survived infancy. For a time all went well and Thomas was created Baron Grey de Wilton in 1784. Sadly, however, they lost their son Thomas and their daughter Frances as children in the 1790s and only the eldest child, Eleanor, lived to see her father created 1st Earl of Wilton in 1801. She married Robert, later Marquess of Westminster. Their first son inherited his father's title but the second, Thomas, born in 1799, became second Earl of Wilton when his grandfather died in 1814.

The second Earl occupied Heaton Park until his death at the age of 83. He was an outstanding figure, especially in horse racing circles, and one of his ideas was to create a 'Goodwood of the North' within his estate. He did establish a racecourse there, but after ten years or so he looked around for another location. Some of the races were moved to Liverpool but the Earl also had land in Radcliffe and the Radcliffe racecourse was a popular rendezvous for many years up to 1876.

The 1870s saw the Earl in dispute with the Lancashire & Yorkshire Railway, who wanted to build a new line which would be passing through Heaton Park. He objected to the smoke belching out from the engines over his beautiful parkland, so they had to construct a tunnel through which the trains would pass.

The Countess Margaret died in 1858, a benevolent and gracious lady. She was responsible for founding St Margaret's Church

at Prestwich and people remembered her driving through the district in a coach drawn by four cream-coloured horses, giving food and clothing to the poor people of the area. During the winter months she opened a soup kitchen at Heaton Hall where unfortunates could have a meal free of charge.

Changing times: a steam tram, with a more modern electric one behind it, 1905

TRANSPORT

From 1846 the people of Bury, and their goods, could be transported more quickly and easily than before. A group of local industrialists had been planning to bring the railway into Bury for two years and on September 28th the station in the centre of town was opened, just behind the old Nelson Inn and the shop of Mr Ambler, a gents' outfitter. By then the company had become the East Lancashire Railway Company and Bolton Street Station became its headquarters. Apparently the coaching companies were so worried that they tried posting men at the top of Bolton Street to direct potential railway passengers to the coach offices!

On the up-line platform arose an imposing edifice, built in neo-classical style with a facade which was dignity itself. A driveway for carriages swept down from the top of Bolton Street and a massive stone staircase was built for pedestrian passengers to walk up to Bank Street and into Silver Street. The staircase is still there, a monument to the strength and skill of Victorian craftsmanship, and the iron balustrade with its uprights elegantly fashioned gives an air of refinement set against the lofty solidarity of the stonework. Seventy years ago I, and many other lads, used to

play 'on th'station steps', a popular game which consisted simply of asking passengers if they had any cigarette cards.

On the opposite side of Bolton Street there was plenty of space for sidings where wagons of goods could be dealt with, so an excellent goods depot and a roomy warehouse with crane power along its staging were built at Castlecroft. I have seen an account dated June 1855 belonging to John Randle, a builder and timber dealer of 8 Water Street. He received a consignment of 6 pine logs from a Mr Bennett of Manchester. The railway invoice from Manchester estimated the weight of the timber at 10 tons and, with carriage charges at 6s8d a ton, the bill came to £3.6.8d. However, the exact weight was taken at Bury and since the money had been paid carriage forward, an overcharge of £1.5.8d was knocked off Mr Randle's account.

The goods depot was very well planned. There was a gate at Castlecroft where carts and lorries could turn right to go down to Bury Bridge, an area where mills and works were constantly increasing, and another gate at School Brow allowed access to Rock Street; no doubt the load of timber for John Randle would pass that way.

Bolton Street Station steps

Water Street had previously been Moorside, but the change of name was more than justified by the amount of water around, much of it draining into the lodges of the many textile mills. For by the mid-19th century Bury had expanded in all quarters to become more than simply a thriving market town. In addition to its original staple trade in woollens, it had attracted many cotton goods manufacturers and these of course needed the services of bleachers, iron and brass founders and engineers. There was also quite an extensive hat making trade. Bury had always had a supply of water from its two rivers and their tributaries, since the 1790s coal had been brought regularly along the canal and the arrival of the railway made the town an ideal place for manufacture.

Tram passing Knowsley Street Station, 1930s

The inventors nearly went one better. The early steam engines were not very reliable on steep gradients and certainly not very clean, with smoke billowing from the engine's funnel. A new idea was to use atmospheric traction and briefly, this was how it was done. A tube was laid between the lines and by pumping out the air in front of a piston a vacuum was created, so that atmospheric pressure drove the piston, and the train to which it was attached, along the tube. In the early 1840s this system was on the verge of becoming a popular method of transport. Four such railways were built and operated public services; Acts of Parliament were obtained to build similar lines, other schemes reached the stage of Parliamentary Bills and still more never got that far.

Joseph Samuda was the inventor and nearly altered the shape of Bury town centre for good. In October 1845 he proposed operating an atmospheric railway from Hunts Bank in Manchester to the Market Place, Bury, with a capital of £200,000, and plans were deposited in November. At the same time he proposed a Rochdale, Heywood and Manchester branch line. But there is no mention of his introducing a Bill to Parliament and presumably the plans only got as far as the Railway Commissioners.

One of Samuda's fiercest opponents was John Herapath, a mathematics tutor who had become interested in railway journalism. He took over the 'Railway Magazine' and eventually converted it into 'Herapath's Railway and

Commercial Journal'. He continually attacked the growth of atmospheric traction and put the blame on the Prime Minister, Sir Robert Peel. In the end, Herapath's criticisms of atmospheric railways were proved right and Bury Market Place remained intact. The atmospheric system depended on an airtight connection between piston and train; the hot summer of 1846 proved too much for the tallow and wax which sealed the valve, no remedy could be found and the idea was abandoned.

In 1883 another method of transporting the people of Bury came into being, the steam tramway. On Monday, 12th March the first tram left the Market Place bound for Whitefield, Prestwich and Kersal. That day three engines and cars made five journeys carrying 700 passengers. Shortly afterwards a horse-car service was started to Limefield but before long steam-propelled vehicles were being used on this route too and people in the surrounding districts were soon enjoying this novel form of public transport.

The service was inaugurated by the Manchester, Bury, Rochdale and Oldham Steam Tramway Company, but the residents of Bury were not entirely satisfied. They complained of the noise, smoke and fumes, and owing to the narrowness of Rock Street the Rector of Bury had obtained a protective clause forbidding trams to proceed along Market Street and Clough Street. There was also a propensity to irregular time-keeping which often caused speeds to be dangerously increased if trams were delayed. So the steam system only lasted about twenty

Trams in Bury town centre, about 1935

years and throughout there was friction between Bury Corporation and the tramway company. Both wanted to introduce an overhead system of electric traction but eventually the Corporation took over the tramways and in 1903 the first electric tram left Moorgate for Jericho. In a matter of two years the borough's electric tramway routes were covering the entire area.

Despite the speed at which the steam trams travelled, there were very few accidents. However, one did occur on Good Friday, 1885. A tram for Rochdale was scheduled to leave the depot in Castle Street at 1.35, but it was held up by ten minutes because another tram from Castle Street to Prestwich had also been delayed. Consequently the Rochdale driver was trying to make up time, and the car was overloaded, with standing passengers on both lower and upper decks. As the tram proceeded along Market Street, Princess Street and King Street, it began rocking and rolling, inducing a state of panic in its passengers. Moving into Rochdale Road, the car turned over on its side with a terrific crash as the panes of glass shattered. The passengers on the top deck were thrown into the roadway and those below were hurled about inside. Miraculously no-one was killed and although some passengers suffered internal injuries and broken limbs, the majority escaped with cuts, sprains, bruises and the inevitable shock to their nervous systems. The conductor received an injury to his hand but the driver was unhurt; in his defence, he claimed he had to exceed the speed limit to make the seven mile trip in the fifty minutes he was allowed.

The tramway scheme went from strength to strength, and some statistics for the year 1911/1912 may be of interest. Fifteen million passengers were carried in 50 cars, 26 tons of copper coin passed through the company's offices and the year's wage bill was £18,000. Lost property for the year was as follows: 376 umbrellas, 72 purses, 2 muffs, 36 books, 60 pairs of gloves, 25 door keys, 5 tobacco pouches, 3 aprons, 12 shirts, 2 towels, 2 pipes, 22 bags, 14 brooches, 25 coats, 2 pairs of spectacles, 5 pictures, 27 walking sticks, 5 scarves, 5 suits of clothes, 2 watches, 2 rings, 2 pairs of scissors, 23 baskets, 7 dinner cans, 2 pairs of boots, 2 hat pins, 2 pairs of stockings, 2 collars, 2 cricket bats, 2 spades and 2 caps. I wonder how that compares with today!

Castle Street, where the steam tram depot was located, probably got its name from the ancient Bury Castle, already well established in mediaeval times. Some of the walls were uncovered in 1865 by workmen making a sewer, and in more recent times Bury Archaeological Group has been able to unearth the northeastern corner buttress and plot the exact site of the castle.

Some of the stones of the castle are said to have been used in the doorway of the Volunteer Armoury, now better known as the Drill Hall. Built in the 1860s, it is somewhat different from most of Bury's Victorian architecture, being in the Norman style. Indeed, people walking up Bolton Street and looking up Cooper Street in earlier days would have been reminded of the castle by the Drill Hall's battlements, clock turret and dogtooth ornamentation. The cornerstone was laid on 22nd August 1868 by R N Philips, Bury's MP, but Castle Street has seen several changes since then. Perhaps the first one was when the building close to the Drill Hall became the depot of the steam trams and the public house opposite changed its name to the Old Bay Horse and Tramway Hotel. In 1906 great alterations took place, including the addition of the tramways premises to the Drill Hall and in 1907 the new extension was opened by the Duke of Connaught, the third son of Queen Victoria.

Eventually it became the headquarters of the Territorial Army and in 1943 there was a disastrous fire and explosion in which the Officers' Mess and storerooms were almost destroyed. Fireman Walter Sunderland was killed and 16 other people injured. Of course, it was wartime and the incident was reported as having occurred 'at a building near the town centre'. Many shops had their windows blown in and some had to close, but one man made the best of the situation. His window was broken but not completely destroyed and he put up a notice saying, 'More Open Than Usual'.

There was a wartime labour shortage and the rebuilding of the Drill Hall was delayed until 1951, when garages and workshops were added. I have not been inside for many years but from the days of my youth I can remember the tremendous floor space available.

Looking up Cooper Street towards the Drill Hall and the Old Bay Horse before the tramways came (see cover)

🝠🝠🝠🝠🝠🝠🝠🝠🝠🝠🝠🝠🝠🝠🝠🝠🝠

CASTLE RINK TO PALAIS GLIDE

Near the back of Bolton Street Station was an area known as Castle Ground, probably because of its proximity to the site of the ancient Bury Castle. At the turn of the century there were one or two industrial concerns here and in 1908 a large, one-storey, wooden building was erected, which I imagine was intended to be a roller skating rink. At that time the roller skating craze had swept through America and spread rapidly to Europe, where rinks were set up in all the major entertainment centres. The nearest one to Bury was Manchester's White City, but it soon became evident that everyone wanted to get in on the roller skating act.

The rink was scheduled to open in the Easter week of 1909 and in the meantime one or two boxing and wrestling matches took place in the hall. By March announcements were appearing in the Bury Times that the Castle Skating Rink Company Ltd (Secretary and Manager, Harry Riley) would be opening for business on Tuesday, 6th April 1909. It was an elaborate introduction, much emphasis being laid upon the 'American rock maple floor' upon which Professor G S Monohan, 'America's greatest fancy and trick skater', diplayed his skills; these included steeplechasing over 9 chairs and skating on a revolving barrel. His advice on how to fall made it all sound very painless: 'Just let your muscles go slack and subside as gracefully as possible'.

Bury had another skating rink, which gives some idea of the impact which the new craze had on the pleasure-seeking popul-ace. The Trafalgar Rink was at

Regal Cinema, Bolton Street, 1951

the corner of Lord Street and South Cross Street (where Hargreaves is now) and was opened in the very same week as the Castle. Previously the Trafalgar Weaving Shed, it had been converted at considerable expense, with the inevitable maple floor covering the flag-stones of the old mill. The pillars supporting the roof could not, of course, be moved and were suitably padded. Both rinks had three sessions daily and the admission prices were the same: no charge in the morning, 6d in the afternoon and 6d in the evening (except that ladies could get in free in the afternoons at the Trafalgar). It cost 1s to hire a pair of skates.

There is little doubt that the advent of moving pictures sounded the death knell of roller skating. Before the First World War the Castle Rink had become the Castle Cinema and the Trafalgar was taken over

by Bentley & Jackson's, engineers. As a cinema, the Castle was unique. Only the best seats at the back were set on a slope so that you could see over the people in front. The cheaper seats were on a flat floor and if you happened to be behind a lady, it was common practice to ask her to remove her hat. The puffing of engines entering or leaving the station and the roar of trains passing through could be heard clearly and were a source of annoyance, particularly when the 'talkies' came and the spoken word was often drowned by the noise. After some years the licence of the Castle was not renewed and in the meantime the Regal Cinema was built on the opposite side of the street.

In 1937 the Castle was closed and the building was purchased by six businessmen, among them Arthur Murray, Johnny Jopson and Oliver Ashworth, who were well known locally. It was their intention to convert it into a Palais-de-Danse and Gliderdrome, that is, a place where people could dance or glide around on roller skates fitted with rubber 'tyres'. During the extensive – and expensive – interior alter-ations, it was discovered that the floorboards which had been laid over the original floor had been worn through by the clog irons of the threepenny-front-seat patrons, resulting in considerable damage to the 'rock maple' underneath. A special machine designed to plane large surfaces had to be hired to level it off. Unfortun-ately, the authorities were loth to grant a licence, insisting that the hall was not suitable

The end of Bury Palais, 1970

for the purpose intended, and there was a long delay. Eventually, after ordering that certain adjacent derelict buildings be demolished, they relented and the Bury Palais-de-Dance opened in August 1939.

The Second World War quickly followed and I cannot recollect roller gliding ever taking place. The Palais did, however, become one of the most popular rendezvous for dancers in the Manchester area and continued to delight young and old for around thirty years. On the opening night it was introduced to Bury by Jack Cannon and his Nine Ritz Boys playing swing. This band was just beginning and soon came to the notice of a wider public,

making their first radio broadcast on 22nd March 1941. 'Smile, Darn You, Smile' became one of the best known signature tunes in the country, a tune which had a special message for all local boys serving in the Forces.

After the war Jack Cannon left the Palais to conquer fresh fields but returned in 1955 and stayed there until his retirement in the early 1960s. In 1964, however, the Palais celebrated 25 years of dancing and on that night he couldn't let down his throng of admirers, young and old, who wanted to hear once again the joyous strains of the past.

Dunn's shop on the corner of Tithebarn Street and the Rock, 1950

ㅁㅁ

BURY JUSTICE: BURY CRIME

In 1927, when I was eighteen, you were never dressed up without a bowler, or 'pot' as they were called, so I saved up and bought one from Dunn's – yes, the shop which is still there at the corner of Tithebarn Street. I think the hat cost 7s6d and periodically I would call in and have it brushed free of charge. Thinking about Dunn's reminded me of the premises on the site in earlier days. The address then was No.1 Rock Street and in 1870 Giles Hewart lived there. He was a silk mercer and linen

draper, and later became a JP. He was also a councillor, first elected for opposing the original, expensive tramway scheme. Bury had already had to pay £45,000 of the £162,000 compensation received by the steam tramways company when the various Corporations took over the trams, and Bury's first Corporation Tramways Committee were about to embark on a scheme which would have cost £285,000 on top of this. But Bury citizens were keeping a close eye on things. They held a town's protest meeting

in 1901, the committee was sacked and the new committee came up with a £186,000 plan. All this, however, was far in the future. In 1870 Giles Hewart's business had only been going three years and he had a baby son to support. Young Gordon, born on 7th January that year, was destined to become one of the greatest advocates in the land.

As Gordon Hewart's education progressed, it became obvious that he had particular qualities and after leaving university and spending a short time as a journalist, he devoted his attention to the law. He was called to the bar in 1902 and subsequently his career embraced a string of successes – K.C, MP for Leicester, a knighthood, solicitor general, Privy Councillor, attorney general and, in 1922, King George V approved his appointment as Lord Chief Justice of England and later conferred a peerage. A reporter who knew him well referred to him as having 'powers of orderly thought and a sense of proportion, a masterful grasp of a principle and skill in applying it to the situation in hand.' He was often referred to as the 'Napoleon of the Bar', yet his force of character never subdued his personal charm. He never forgot his home town and visited as often as he could to lecture on many subjects. Nor was he pompous or conceited. In 1912, before gaining the Parliamentary seat for Leicester, he stood as a Liberal candidate for North West Manchester and

Campaigning for Gordon Hewart in Stevenson Square, Manchester, 2/8/1912

lost. In 1929 the city held a civic reception for him and he visited it for the first time since being made Lord Chief Justice. In his speech he referred to his former failure and made a joke about Manchester preferring his legal skills to his political ones.

I am old enough to remember the sensational Sandhills Murder at St Anne's which occurred on Christmas Eve 1919. It caused great excitement in the area, and particularly in Bury when it was discovered that the defendant was a native of Holcombe. The trial was at Manchester Assizes with Sir Gordon Hewart (as he was then) representing the Crown – yet another cause for local interest.

The victim was Kathleen Breaks, an attractive and fashionably dressed woman who was stabbed and shot to death. She was married but living apart from her husband and had been associated for some time with Frederick Holt, an ex-Army officer of independent means who was eventually charged with her murder.

The case was a notable example of Sir Gordon's precise conduct, and the logical and imperturbable manner in which facts were built up against the accused was unassailable even by the skills of Sir Edward Marshall Hall, K.C, defending.

In his summing up, however, Sir Gordon roundly criticised the melodramatic behaviour of many women who crowded the public gallery of the court, asking them to look a little more compassionately on the unfortunate victim. She had fallen for a rotter who, under the guise of a lover, had planned diabolically to insure her life and murder her to get the benefit. Holt was found guilty and sentenced to death. Not the 'crime of the century' by any means, but the close affinity to Bury and district made it a local sensation.

A Bury witness was called when the case went to appeal in 1920. Holt had originally tried to enter a plea of insanity but the jury had decided he was fit to plead and he had changed this to 'Not Guilty'. At the appeal hearing the question of his mental health was brought up again and Mrs Amy Worsley of Brandlesholme was called. She had been a servant of Holt's maternal grandfather, Mr Richard Rothwell of Brandlesholme Old Hall, in the 1870s and described how Mr Rothwell had delusions that people were trying to poison him, refusing to eat unless someone else tasted the food first. Not surprisingly, the link with Holt was considered a little tenuous and the court ruled that the execution must go ahead.

Thirty years earlier, Bury did have its 'crime of the century', referred to in national newspapers as 'The Bury Wardrobe Murder'. It happened at No.39 Bolton Street, the well stocked Gordon Furnishing Company. The owners were a Jewish family whose business was based in Manchester, with one or two branches around Lancashire; the head of the firm, Samuel Gordon, had two sons, George and Meyer. At the Bury shop they employed a manager named William Dukes, a man between 25 and 30 years of age who had had a somewhat unsettled career. Among other things, he had been a solicitor's clerk in Bolton and he and his wife lived in North Street, Bury, where they kept a small confectioner's shop. He was well known at the Admiral Lord Nelson pub just up the road at No.29 and appears to have had something of a drink problem; at any rate he had been sacked by his previous employer for visiting a barmaid during business hours.

George Gordon often came to Bury to look over the books and settle up business matters, but for about five weeks Dukes had postponed his employer's visit, saying that he was needed in Manchester to meet a customer who was looking to spend some £60. But the customer never came and on the Wednesday morning of September 25th 1889, George Gordon arrived for his usual purpose. Since he had to be back in Manchester to celebrate the Jewish New Year, Mr Gordon was very annoyed to find Dukes absent, and was heard to say that he would return in the afternoon and not leave Bury until he had seen Dukes.

He saw him early in the afternoon, a load of furniture arrived and Tootill (the boy assistant) and the carrier were told by Dukes to take it to Lime Tree House, Prestwich. They set off about ten minutes to three, leaving George Gordon and Dukes together on the premises. Gordon should have been back in Manchester at six o'clock for a New Year service, but he never arrived.

It was most uncharacteristic of George Gordon to miss the evening festival on Jewish New Year and on the Thursday morning his father and his brother Meyer set off to Bury to discover his whereabouts. Dukes said he had probably gone to Burnley, where the firm had another branch, but this proved not to be the case. Meyer Gordon was beginning to get apprehensive and reported

Nos 33-43 Bolton Street

his brother missing to the police.

They were not very co-operative, thinking he would turn up sooner or later, but Meyer persisted and eventually, after much argument, Superintendent Henderson agreed to send two constables to search the shop premises.

At first, nothing appeared to be out of the ordinary but Meyer Gordon spotted a painted wardrobe, about 5' in height, and he insisted on it being opened. Dukes said he didn't know where the key was, so the police forced it open. Inside they found George Gordon's body doubled up, face down and wrapped in a quantity of packing and an old hearthrug. Dukes was callously cool and collected, standing by with hands in his pockets and seemingly unaffected by the discovery. In his excitement, Meyer Gordon made for him but was held back by a constable. 'So you have murdered my brother!' he exclaimed.

'It's not me that has done that,' replied Dukes, but he was immediately arrested.

When the body was unwrapped at the police station, stiff and cold, a ghastly sight presented itself. The head and neck were a mass of wounds and a blood-stained hammer, chisel and pickaxe were also in the wardrobe. In order to remove suspicion from himself and make it appear that the accounts were in good order, Dukes had forged a letter to himself, purporting to come from J Alstead of Lime Tree House, Prestwich, and promising to send him some money. It was to be his undoing, for it proved that the murder was premeditated.

The entire country was shocked and quickly the proprietors of Madame Tussaud's Exhibition in London endeavoured to secure the wardrobe in which the body of the deceased was concealed as an item for their 'Chamber of Horrors'.

Dukes stood trial on December 4th at Manchester Assizes and was cool and calculated to the end. The jury was out for only 15 minutes and the verdict was 'Guilty of wilful murder'. He was hanged on the morning of Christmas Eve at Strangeways Gaol, Manchester.

THE NEW CENTURY

As the 19th century moved into the 20th, many changes were to take place. The canal was busy, coal shipped from Lady-shore was unloaded at Bury Bridge, the East Lancashire Railway goods yard at Castle-croft was a hive of industry and the passenger trains from across the street were quick and regular. Shops in the Rock prospered as the new era dawned.

The deeds of the Lancashire Fusiliers figure largely in the pages of military history and Bury is proud of its association with the regiment. For many years its depot was the Wellington Barracks in Bolton Road and the rhythm of marching feet was heard regularly throughout the town. The primrose yellow hackle on the head-dress was an honour awarded in 1901 for the regiment's heroic stand the year before at Spion Kop, one of the operations working towards the relief of Ladysmith. Spion Kop itself was a disaster, largely because of mismanagement by the army commanders, and many were killed – of one company which went up 80 strong, only 10 men returned. But General Buller's despatch commended the way in which the Lancashire Fusiliers 'magnificently upheld the best traditions of the British Army'. About a month later, on 28th February, Ladysmith was relieved after 119 days of siege by the Boers; the news reached Bury about dinner time on Thursday, 1st March.

The people of Bury were delighted; 'their' regiment's sacrifice had not been in vain and once again the Lancashire Fusiliers had played a major part in the nation's victory. But at that time Bury citizens had a double cause for rejoicing and, to be honest, many of them were more concerned with sporting achievements nearer home – Bury Football Club was matched with Sheffield United in a replay FA Cup tie at Gigg Lane.

Nearly everybody in town went to the match, in fact the crowd was so great that they broke into the ground and large numbers got in without paying. Many of the mills were stopped to mark the relief of Ladysmith and in others, men had worked overtime so that they could have the afternoon off. A memorable day: Sheffield United lost 2-0 and Bury went on to win the Cup.

The South African War ended in 1902 and in recognition of the distinguished service of the Lancashire Fusiliers, a lasting memorial to fallen comrades was erected by all ranks and friends of the regiment. The celebrated sculptor George

Marching feet: a military procession in Bolton Street

Frampton was commissioned to supply a suitable statue and his eight-foot bronze figure of a Lancashire Fusilier shows him in an attitude of victory, rifle and bayonet handy and busby aloft, waved in triumph. Upstanding on an appropriate pedestal and facing in exaltation along Market Street, it was erected where the lamp used to be in the centre of the Market Place. Frampton's portrayal of the joy of victory was a refreshing change from the misery of war typical of so many sculptured pieces. About that time he became a member of the Royal Academy and was knighted in 1908.

Wellington Barracks, Bolton Road, Bury

The Fusilier was completed in 1905 and the unveiling ceremony was performed by Lord Derby, wearing his Lord Lieutenant's uniform. In his acceptance speech the Mayor, Alderman Butcher, promised to preserve the memorial and keep it in good condition. After the ceremony the troops, with their colourful scarlet and blue uniforms, paraded to the Drill Hall for refreshments, and to mark the occasion an old folks' treat was held later in the day.

June 1914 saw the completion of the Whitehead Memorial Clock Tower and Gardens, presented to the town by Mr Henry Whitehead in memory of his brother Walter, an eminent surgeon of Manchester. The opening ceremony was performed

by another famous surgeon, Sir Frederick Treves and Mr Whitehead's young grandson John started the clock. The erection of the Portland stone memorial tower by F M & H Nuttall of Whitefield brought a stateliness and beauty to the town's entrance from the south, and to include the South African warrior in the scheme was an opportunity not to be missed. Unfortunately the Great War intervened and it was not until 1920 that the South African war memorial was transferred to its new site in Whitehead Gardens. Then, of course, there was a vacant space in the Market Place and by this time Bury's electric tram system was

operating to the outskirts of the town and the Market Place was as busy as a railway junction. There was not a lot of room, but it was decided to install a shelter for the convenience of waiting passengers and it became something of a joke among the townspeople. It had a good roof but no sides and it was a bit uncomfortable if the rain was blowing slantingly. Like the lamp of earlier days, though, it was still a central meeting place and I will wager that many local married couples started their assignations under the old 'umbrella'.

I was born early in the present century and have very clear memories of the years between the wars. When the Great War ended I was getting old enough to wander around Bury with other lads and there were many attractions. Even more lucrative than hanging about 'on th'station steps' in the hope of getting cigarette cards was the following procedure. We would obtain a broom stick, put soft soap on the end of it and wander around the Market Place looking for coins that had been dropped through gratings. Put the pole through the bars and the soft soap would stick to anything useful and bring it up.

I enjoyed playing football but I wasn't very good – I was too small. Nevertheless, I was in the house team at the Junior Day Technical School in Broad Street, where I went for two years in my early teens. Our field was in front of the Peel Mills and we had to strip in the school and walk down Castlecroft to play. We even had to make our own goal-posts in woodwork classes and carry

Bury Market Place, March 1905. The South African War Memorial is about to be unveiled, but the triumphant busby can already be seen

them down to the ground. At the corner of Castlecroft was a sports and athletic outfitter called William N Nuttall and I visited him frequently to buy football-boot studs, laces, dubbin, shin-guards and, occasionally, knickers. Even when I left school he remained my supplier, for I started work as a messenger boy at the railway goods yard at Knowsley Street and four times a day I had to walk through Bolton Street with messages from and to the old East Lancashire yard at Castlecroft. Nearly every dinner time the clerks would require me to call for a meat pie or a cake from Preston & Company, the luncheon and tea rooms close to Bolton Street Station. I knew the place very well and in later years learned the story of the proprietor's beginnings.

'Th'Umbrella'

The founding Preston was James, married in 1874 to Miss Annie Graves, the eldest daughter of a confectioner in Rock Street. At that time James Preston was a manager at Kirklees Printworks in Tottington but when his father-in-law retired, he bought the shop and later another confectionery business in Bolton Street. He ran both until his own retirement in 1922, by which time his only son Hubert and daughter-in-law Maggie had come into the business and Prestons owned another shop in Fleet Street. Unfortunately Hubert died rather young, but Maggie kept going for some years at the Rock Street shop, which became known as M Preston's.

She had acquired a cake recipe from her late husband and became the pioneer of the Bury simnel cake trade, sending her products to Bury businessmen the world over.

Simnel cake was nothing new, of course; it dates back 300 years or so, when it was the custom to offer it to friends and neighbours on mid-Lent Sunday. The name is thought to derive from the Latin simila, a fine flour. The original Bury simnel is attributed to Lydia Hutchinson; in the late 18th century she and her husband Robert were the only confectioners in Bury and not another simnel cake was known to exist anywhere.

I wasn't a messenger for long and was promoted to the E.L. There was a weighbridge and a brick-built cabin just outside the gates and I had it to myself, weighing carts and lorries - and there were plenty of them. It had a great crane operated by two men turning a crank handle attached to a ratchet which engaged on a huge gear wheel: a slow operation, but it could deal effectively with the steel girders from Webb's, the enormous drying cylinders used in papermaking from Charlie Walmsley's and the huge tree trunks for the Wormald Timber Company which used to be behind the Black Bull Inn in Stanley Street. They specialised in home-grown timber, particularly sycamore, and during the Great War supplied planks for the decks of landing craft.

As you turned into Castlecroft the Congregational Chapel was on the right and the old Napier Inn on the left, built in the 1850s. When Mr R N Philips was celebrating his election as MP for Bury, Admiral Sir Charles Napier was one of the visiting speakers. He was well received by the people of Bury and it seems likely that the Napier Inn was named after him.

Bolton Street has changed immensely but the old Temperance Billiard Hall with its two vaults and green exterior is still there. (Identical halls could be seen in other Lancashire towns at one time.) It was a very popular rendezvous for the youth of the area and remained a billiard hall for many years before being used by other businesses; today it is the Bury Snooker Club.

Whitehead Gardens, 1955, the second site for the Lancashire Fusilier's statue

OLD FLEET STREET

Everyone knew there were four different streets from the Market Place to Moorside (Fleet Street, Rock Street, Stanley Street and Water Street), but we all called it 'The Rock', a thoroughfare teeming with shoppers looking around for butchers, bakers and candlestick makers. Everything you wanted was there – and still is, but as I look around today I try to recall the old establishments I knew sixty years ago. Marks & Spencers is still in Bury, at the end of Union Arcade, but what a difference! The old place on Fleet Street had just two stalls, selling nothing more than a penny. There was no door, you could just walk in and out with your meagre, but necessary, requirements. The shop was closed at night with a roller of iron slats which could be pulled up and down.

Marks & Spencer's Penny Bazaar was at 52 Fleet Street and at No.48 was E A Bostock, a boot and shoe shop established as long ago as 1885. In 1889 John Bostock and his wife Elizabeth Ann took over the business from the founder, John's brother, and the family were to sell boots and shoes there for over 100 years. John himself died nine years later at the early age of 41, but Elizabeth Ann took over the running of the business, eventually altering the name to E A Bostock.

The Rock, with Marks & Spencer's and Read, Franklin & Heywood's, behind the bus

Elizabeth's eldest son, John Livingstone Bostock, spent his life at the shop, in his younger days working in the basement repairing boots and fitting clog irons, for the Bostocks also provided a cobbling service. He knew the trade inside out and was well respected by his competitors and an influential citizen of Bury with wide interests.

One of his most successful lines was the Kiltie brand of shoes for children which became famous when his twin sons, Dennis and Michael, were born sixty-odd years ago. When they were nine months old, the two lads were photographed for a Kiltie advertisement saying, 'Every Pair Alike'.

John L lived to the great age of 84 and three of his sons followed the trade until their own retirements. Geoffrey was manager of four shoe factories in Norwich and Dennis and Michael ran the Bury establishment until the 99-year lease on the property ran out. However, the 'Kiltie twins' of Bury were reborn not so long ago, when the Leicester-based Portland Shoes, who had acquired the brand, started to use the old black and white picture for promotion purposes. Dennis and Michael were said to be 'highly delighted'.

Many people will remember the twins' mother, Mrs Lizzie Bostock, for her untiring efforts on behalf of various Bury charities. Among other things, she was Vice-President of Bury British Legion and organised

Bostock's shop on Fleet Street, 1903

the British Legion Poppy Day collectors for six years up to 1948, and for 21 years she was a Welfare Officer for Bury Red Cross, running a parcel service to prisoners-of-war as part of her duties.

Between Bostock's and Marks & Spencer was a shop occupied for many years (until Marks expanded) by Rawson & Grimshaw, clothiers and at No.46 were Read and Franklin, practical piano workmen. In 1913 they combined businesses with Gilbert Heywood and altered the name to the famous Read, Franklin & Heywood – still going after 75 years, but now in Broad Street. Gilbert Heywood came from a long-established Heywood family. His grandfather John founded the Heywood Advertiser in 1855 and his father, Edward W, was a well known music dealer and for ten years organist at St Paul's Church.

The Rock, 1958. From right to left the picture shows: Williams Deacons Bank, Downham's ironmonger's, Alexandre tailor's, Van Allan, Read Franklin & Heywood, Bostock's

In 1891 Joseph Downham had built the large, double-fronted shop which turned the corner into Union Street. Downhams were general ironmongers who could provide everything necessary for mill furnishing as well as speciality tools for engineers, moulders and others. Fifty years earlier there had been several small shops on this corner, one of them owned by Henry Peel, who had another shop in the Corn Market. (Broad Street will tell you where the Corn Market was, near the site of Lord Derby's first market, built in 1839.) On 1st January 1853 Henry Peel sold up and Joseph Downham took over the business, which prospered.

Not long afterwards Robert Hall and Henry Turner came into the business with him, and by 1913 all the shares were held by the Hall and Turner families. Joseph Downham himself had died in 1896 but the name was kept, and until comparatively recently Downham's was a household word for ironmongery in Bury. In 1969 they linked up with John Kay & Sons (Bury) Ltd and in the 1970s their portion of the Rock was redeveloped. The old building on the corner of Union Street was demolished to make way for a pedestrianisation project. Such is progress!

Incidentally, Joseph Downham's father, a cabinet maker also named Joseph, died in 1869 and was the first person to be buried in Bury Cemetery, opened in May of that year.

One of the most interesting shops along Fleet Street was the jeweller's known as Lepp's. The firm goes back to 1836 when Matthew Waldvogel, a clockmaker and dealer, came to Bury and opened a shop in Stanley Street. He carried on business there for some years, but by 1871 had moved into Rock Street and was calling his business Waldvogel & Co, watchmakers and jewellers. In 1905 Mr J D Lepp purchased the company and after more than half a century his name is still there. He died in 1957 at the age of 86 and had been one of Bury's most influential councillors and Mayor of Bury in 1928/29.

Finally, one cannot forget Lipton's. It stood opposite Union Street, which joined up with Spring Street, and you could stand in Heywood Street and look right along this lengthy thoroughfare to see Lipton's in Fleet Street. I remember it chiefly for its cellars, from which we were allowed to take the empty boxes to chop up for firewood – but I've told that story elsewhere.

Engraving of Downham's shop in its heyday

ROCK STREET AND BEYOND

Fleet Street ended at Tithebarn Street, a name which derives from the days when the tithe-hay received from the Rector's glebe lands was stored in a barn at the Rectory. Rock Street continued along to Eden Street and on the corner of Tithebarn Street was John Crisp & Co, hosier and glover; a pal of mine from the 'Tech' started work in that little shop in 1924. We had to call out our own names in the roll call and Campbell and Fletcher were close. We had the same desk, the same woodwork bench and the two vices next to each other in the metalwork shop, where we filed hopelessly in an attempt to form the metal into a specified shape.

Anyhow, Sam Fletcher got a job at Crisp's and later moved to Bradshaw's, a larger men's outfitter's in Princess Street. Mr Robert Bradshaw was an ideal tutor, widely respected as a magistrate in both town and county; he was for many years Chairman of Bury Borough Juvenile Magistrates until his retirement in 1964. The Queen is the Duke of Lancaster and when the Duchy's 700th anniversary celebrations were held in 1965, Mr Robert Bradshaw was presented to the Queen at Buckingham Palace, in recognition of his special services to the Duchy.

After twelve years, Sam Fletcher had done so well at Bradshaw's that he was able to establish his own business of high-class gents' outfitting. His shop was

Bradshaw's shop on the corner of a busy Princess Street

in Haymarket Street for many years and his son John eventually took over; today the old family firm still carries on in Union Street. Sam's father, Mr L Fletcher, was a top class referee and was regularly in action at Football League fixtures; rather surprising, therefore, that I never saw Sam playing in the school's games.

Turning into Tithebarn Street is School Brow, where Harvey's tannery used to be. The tan

pits were started in 1814 by John Peel and apparently his two sons and a daughter founded Peel Tannery (Henry Peel, the ironmonger I mentioned earlier, may have been one of this family). Matthew Peel, the last of them to run the tannery, served as one of Bury's Improvement Commissioners for nearly thirty years and then as a councillor for Elton Ward from 1876 until his death.

In 1870 three Harvey brothers,

Peel Tannery

Matthew Peel

Guy, William and Jesse, bought the business from him and 12 years later one of the brothers purchased another tannery in Nantwich; the two companies merged in 1899 and the firm flourished for nearly 60 more years. After the Second World War, Bernard, Guy's son, took over and Harvey's remained a household word, in Bury at least. In 1957, however, Bernard died at the age of 70 and the Bury works was closed.

In the old days Rock Street was very narrow; indeed, the whole area was so compact that people could not move around freely. On the corner of Eden Street was Heap & Son Ltd, probably Bury's foremost fashion store with five windows of ladies' and gents' London and Paris creations and the products of Britain's best looms in the drapery and house furnishing departments. I got my first long trousers there (a memorable occasion, for in those days boys wore short trousers until they left school). Across the road were Clough Street and the 86-year-old Roe Buck Hotel, which earlier still was called the Buck and Joiner's Arms. Between there and Cross Street was a row of ancient shops which projected almost into the middle of the roadway, so that trams moving into Clough Street had to encroach about a foot on to the pavement. So narrow were the footpaths of Rock Street that pedestrians often had to step into the road.

In 1933, however, the pub and the shops were demolished and Hornby Buildings, a splendid example of municipal enterprise, arose about 50 feet further

Rock Street, c1910, the site of Hornby Buildings. Winterhalter's jeweller's was at No.32, Disney's at 30, R Norris at 28 and John Stone's pork butcher's at 24

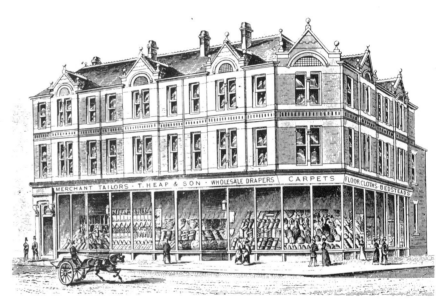

Drawing of T Heap & Son, 1903

The Rock, c1905. J D Lepp's jeweller's is on the right at No.22, next to C Benton, tobacconist. At No. 26 is J Brown's, then Greenhalgh's confectioner's, next to Parker Walker's tripe shop

back. The new building had a distinctive appeal of its own and after it opened on October 14th, floodlights shone on the facade for a fortnight. The light-coloured stonework and the coat of arms of the borough in full colour brought an unaccustomed brightness to the area. The building was named in honour of the Hornby family's association with the town. For the previous three years the Rector of Bury had been the Rt Rev H L Hornby, who was to stay for another twenty until his retirement in 1953; for part of that time he was also Bishop of Hulme. Two of his earlier kinsmen had also been Rectors of Bury, Geoffrey (1818–1850) and his son Edward (1850–1888), and several of the town's streets were named after members of the Hornby family.

Many will remember the traders

in those little shops which were demolished in 1933: Peter Rowe, fishmonger; Winterhalter, jeweller; Walter Baxendale, jeweller; Waller & Riley, chemists; John Stone, pork butcher. John Stone's, now H Stone, is still there, almost on the same spot where the family's business was started about 1860 - a splendid record.

Beyond Rock Street was Stanley Street, home of the renowned Rushworth's Restaurant. Dinners, teas and suppers were supplied and mid-day workers were welcome at the downstairs tables; the office staff upstairs were rather more sedate. In the evenings socials, whist drives and other functions were catered for.

We never had much money in our house, but my parents managed to send me to the 'Tech'; 15s per term. Very often I would meet my mother at Rushworth's and we would have our dinner there, and one day when I was waiting for her a lad from the Tech was passing and stopped to chat. My mother spotted us and kept herself in the background until my friend had taken his leave; she knew that her clogs and shawl would have been an embarrassment to us all.

A little further on, in Moorgate, was Lever's. Mr Lever was a well established pawnbroker and was still there until 1967, when he went into the licensing trade at the Waterloo Hotel in Manchester Road. He retired in 1972 and he and his wife Doris went to live in Tottington. Doris had been Mrs Jones, landlady of the Swan Hotel, Tottington Road, and I happened to be researching that old tavern at the time. The landlord, Wilfred Stanley, put

Mr Lever's pub, the Waterloo Hotel, Manchester Road

Hornby Buildings, illuminated for the Jubilee of King George V in 1936

me in touch with Doris and I had a very pleasant chat with her and Mr Lever. She recalled the crumbling walls of the old Swan and laughingly remembered the 'Nanny Pen' - the nickname older regulars gave to the long, narrow front bar. The new building was erected along the lines of the old foundations as far as possible, and in fact the present tap room is in exactly the same position as the old one.

The old Swan wasn't built as a pub at all, but as a house, by William Millett. It bore a datestone which read 'Millett - William and Ann - 1703'. They were related to the Milletts who ran the bleachworks on the Island and Dr Goodlad was their family doctor. Eventually the estate went to his family,

Mrs Lever's pub, the Swan Hotel, Tottington Road

hence the name of nearby Goodlad Street.

In my teens I used to enjoy a drink with my mates at Herbert Hinchliffe's herbalist's shop at 51 Stanley Street. I think it was Herbert's two sisters who ran it; his works was in a back street off Heywood Street. There he made up every type of herb preparation but his most famous was Hinchliffe's Royal Blood Wine. We used to have sarsaparilla bitters, good for the blood or, if it was very cold, a glass of hot Vimto.

Herbert Hinchliffe was one of my father's oldest friends and in my schooldays I was often sent to his works on Saturday morning with messages – usually, I imagine, bets on racehorses. There were no betting shops in those days and their bookmakers were in the pubs, in this case probably the Boars Head on Water Street. Later, Herbert bought the premises close by, where J & J Clemishaw, drysalters, had been for many years and turned it into a high class wine shop. He had a splendid selection of his usual herbal brands, together with wines and spirits in a business which was taken over in the 1930s by Billy Elliott, another of his compatriots.

Some years later Billy was elected councillor and for ten years helped to run things in Bury. He became an alderman and in 1956/57 was Mayor of Bury. The next Mayor in 1957/58 was James Isherwood,

Clemishaw's drysalter's on the corner of Water Street and Bambury Street

landlord of the Two Tubs and one of the most important personalities in the town. Unfortunately he wasn't in the best of health, so Billy Elliott, throughout a second year, deputised for him at many important meetings and social functions.

To go back to the thirties, when I was about nineteen I was courting strongly, but the railway didn't worry about that. They sent me to Bradford and for 4½ years I didn't know much about Bury. I came home

every weekend, of course, and after 2½ years Emmie and I decided to get married. We had accumulated quite a large 'bottom drawer': the double bed I slept in at home; an upright piano, a gift from Emmie's family; bedding; pots and pans; ornaments and so on – a bit of a problem getting them to Bradford. There wasn't enough for a full scale removal van, so my father asked Billy Elliott if he could assist. He had a herbal brewery wagon and he agreed to do the job.

We cut short our honeymoon in Colwyn Bay to four days and on the Thursday morning we set off. We couldn't manage the piano, in fact it never got to Bradford at all; the cost of packing and transport was prohibitive. There was room for two in the cab besides the driver, but at the last minute my brand new mother-in-law could not resist coming with us, so I had to climb on to the top of the load and looking something like 'Muldoon's picnic', we set out for our new home. Billy did a great job that day, and I believe he also enjoyed the trip.

The Boar's Head on Water Street, where I suspect my father's bookmaker conducted his business

****

For a current list of local history titles available by post, please send a stamped addressed envelope to Neil Richardson, 88 Ringley Road, Stoneclough, Radcliffe, Manchester M26 9ET.

****